A
Semantic Web
Primer

Cooperative Information Systems
Michael P. Papazoglou, Joachim W. Schmidt, and John Mylopoulos, editors

Foundations of Neural Networks, Fuzzy Systems, and Knowledge Engineering
Nikola K. Kasabov, 1996

Advances in Object-Oriented Data Modeling
Michael P. Papazoglou, Stefano Spaccapietra, and Zahir Tari, editors, 2000

Workflow Management: Models, Methods, and Systems
Wil van der Aalst and Kees Max van Hee, 2002

A Semantic Web Primer
Grigoris Antoniou and Frank van Harmelen, 2004

Aligning Modern Business Processes and Legacy Systems
Willem-Jan van den Heuvel, 2006

A Semantic Web Primer, second edition
Grigoris Antoniou and Frank van Harmelen, 2008

Service-Oriented Computing
Dimitrios Georgakopoulos and Mike P. Papazoglou, editors, 2008

At Your Service: Service-Oriented Computing from an EU Perspective
Elisabetta Di Nitto, Anne-Marie Sassen, Paolo Traverso and Arian Zwegers, editors, 2009

Metamodeling for Method Engineering
Manfred A. Jeusfeld, Matthias Jarke and John Mylopoulos, editors, 2009

Social Modeling for Requirements Engineering
Eric Yu, Paolo Giorgini, Neil Maiden and John Mylopoulos, ediorts, 2011

Modeling Business Processes: A Petri Net-Oriented Approach
Wil van der Aalst and Christian Stahl, 2011

A Semantic Web Primer, third edition
Grigoris Antoniou, Paul Groth, Frank van Harmelen and Rinke Hoekstra, 2012

A
Semantic Web
Primer
third edition

Grigoris Antoniou

Paul Groth

Frank van Harmelen

Rinke Hoekstra

The MIT Press
Cambridge, Massachusetts
London, England

This book was set in 10/13 Palatino by the authors using LaTeX 2_ε.
Printed and bound in the United States of America.

Library of Congress Cataloging-in-Publication Data

Antoniou, G. (Grigoris)
A Semantic Web primer / Grigoris Antoniou ... [et al.]. – 3rd ed.
    p. cm. – (Cooperative information systems)
Rev ed. of: A Semantic Web primer / by Grigoris Antoniou. 2nd ed., c2008.
Includes bibliographical references and index.
ISBN 978-0-262-01828-9 (hardcover : alk. paper)
1. Semantic Web. I. Antoniou, G. (Grigoris) II. Antoniou, G. (Grigoris) Semantic Web primer.
TK5105.88815.A58   2012
025.04'27–dc23

                                2012008455

10 9 8 7 6 5 4 3 2 1

To Konstantina, Vangelis and Giorgos

G.A.

To Thomas Groth - Professor

P.G.

Contents

List of Figures

Series Foreword

The traditional view of information systems as tailor-made, cost-intensive database applications is changing rapidly. The change is fueled partly by a maturing software industry, which is making greater use of off-the-shelf generic components and standard software solutions, and partly by the onslaught of the information revolution. In turn, this change has resulted in a new set of demands for information services that are homogeneous in their presentation and interaction patterns, open in their software architecture, and global in their scope. The demands have come mostly from application domains such as e-commerce and banking, manufacturing (including the software industry itself), training, education, and environmental management, to mention just a few.

Future information systems will have to support smooth interaction with a large variety of independent multivendor data sources and legacy applications, running on heterogeneous platforms and distributed information networks. Metadata will play a crucial role in describing the contents of such data sources and in facilitating their integration.

As well, a greater variety of community-oriented interaction patterns will have to be supported by next-generation information systems. Such interactions may involve navigation, querying and retrieval, and will have to be combined with personalized notification, annotation, and profiling mechanisms. Such interactions will also have to be intelligently interfaced with application software, and will need to be dynamically integrated into customized and highly connected cooperative environments. Moreover, the massive investments in information resources, by governments and businesses alike, call for specific measures that ensure security, privacy, and accuracy of their contents.

All these are challenges for the next generation of information systems. We call such systems *cooperative information systems*, and they are the focus of this series.

In lay terms, cooperative information systems are serving a diverse mix of demands characterized by *content—community—commerce*. These demands are originating in current trends for off-the-shelf software solutions, such as enterprise resource planning and e-commerce systems.

A major challenge in building cooperative information systems is to develop technologies that permit continuous enhancement and evolution of current massive investments in information resources and systems. Such technologies must offer an appropriate infrastructure that supports not only development but also evolution of software.

Early research results on cooperative information systems are becoming the core technology for community-oriented information portals or gateways. An information gateway provides a "one-stop-shopping" place for a wide range of information resources and services, thereby creating a loyal user community.

The research advances that will lead to cooperative information systems will not come from any single research area within the field of information technology. Database and knowledge-based systems, distributed systems, groupware, and graphical user interfaces have all matured as technologies. While further enhancements for individual technologies are desirable, the greatest leverage for technological advancement is expected to come from their evolution into a seamless technology for building and managing cooperative information systems.

The MIT Press Cooperative Information Systems series will cover this area through textbooks, and research editions intended for the researcher and the professional who wishes to remain up to date on current developments and future trends.

The series will include three types of books:

- Textbooks or resource books intended for upper-level undergraduate or graduate level courses

- Research monographs, which collect and summarize research results and development experiences over a number of years

- Edited volumes, including collections of papers on a particular topic

Authors are invited to submit to the series editors book proposals that include a table of contents and sample book chapters. All submissions will be reviewed formally and authors will receive feedback on their proposals.

Data in a data source are useful because they model some part of the real world, its subject matter (or *application*, or *domain of discourse*). The problem of *data semantics* is establishing and maintaining the correspondence between a data source, hereafter a *model*, and its intended subject matter. The model may be a database storing data about employees in a company, a database schema describing parts, projects, and suppliers, a website presenting information about a university, or a plain text file describing the battle of Waterloo. The problem has been with us since the development of the first databases. However, the problem remained under control as long as the operational environment of a database remained closed and relatively stable. In such a setting, the meaning of the data was factored out from the database proper and entrusted to the small group of regular users and application programs.

The advent of the web has changed all that. Databases today are made available, in some form, on the web where users, application programs, and uses are open-ended and ever changing. In such a setting, the semantics of the data has to be made available along with the data. For human users, this is done through an appropriate choice of presentation format. For application programs, however, this semantics has to be provided in a formal and machine-processable form. Hence the call for the Semantic Web.[1]

Not surprisingly, this call by Tim Berners-Lee has received tremendous attention by researchers and practitioners alike. There is now an International Semantic Web Conference series,[2] a Semantic Web Journal published by Elsevier,[3] as well as industrial committees that are looking at the first generation of standards for the Semantic Web.

The current book constitutes a timely publication, given the fast-moving nature of Semantic Web concepts, technologies, and standards. The book offers a gentle introduction to Semantic Web concepts, including XML, DTDs, and XML schemas, RDF and RDFS, OWL, logic, and inference. Throughout, the book includes examples and applications to illustrate the use of concepts.

We are pleased to include this book on the Semantic Web in the series on Cooperative Information Systems. We hope that readers will find it interesting, insightful, and useful.

John Mylopoulos	Michael Papazoglou
jm@cs.toronto.edu	M.P.Papazoglou@kub.nl
Dept. of Computer Science	INFOLAB
University of Toronto	P.O. Box 90153
Toronto, Ontario	LE Tilburg
Canada	The Netherlands

---

[1] Tim Berners-Lee and Mark Fischetti, *Weaving the Web: The Original Design and Ultimate Destiny of the World Wide Web by Its Inventor*. San Francisco: HarperCollins, 1999.

[2] iswc.semanticweb.org.

[3] www.semanticwebjournal.org.

Chapter 1

The Semantic Web Vision

1.1 Introduction

1.1.1 Motivation for the Semantic Web

The general vision of a "semantic web" can be summarized in a single phrase: *to make the web more accessible to computers*. The current web is a web of text and pictures. Such media are very useful for people, but computers play a very limited role on the current web: they index keywords, and they ship information from servers to clients, but that is all. All the intelligent work (selecting, combining, aggregating, etc.) has to be done by the human reader. What if we could make the web richer for machines, so that it would be full of machine readable, machine "understandable" *data*? Such a web would facilitate many things that are impossible on the current web: *Search* would be no longer limited to simply looking for keywords, but could become more semantic, which would include looking for synonyms, being aware of homonyms, and taking into account context and purpose of the search query. Websites could become more *personalized* if personal browsing agents were able to understand the contents of a web page and tailor it to personal interest profiles. *Linking* could become more

1

semantic by deciding dynamically which pages would be useful destinations, based on the current user's activities, instead of having to hardwire the same links for all users ahead of time. It would be possible to *integrate* information across websites, instead of users currently having to do a "mental copy-paste" whenever they find some information on one site that they want to combine with information from another.

1.1.2   Design Decisions for the Semantic Web

There are many ways of going about building a more "semantic" web. One way would be to build a "Giga Google," relying on "the unreasonable effectiveness of data"[1] to find the right correlations among words, between terms and context, etc. The plateau in search engine performance that we have been witnessing over the past few years seems to suggest that there are limitations to this approach: none of the search giants have been able to go beyond returning simply flat lists of disconnected pages.

The Semantic Web (or The Web of Data, as it is becoming known in recent years[2]) follows different design principles, which can be summarized as follows:

1. make structured and semi-structured data available in standardized formats on the web;

2. make not just the datasets, but also the individual data-elements and their relations accessible on the web;

3. describe the intended semantics of such data in a formalism, so that this intended semantics can be processed by machines.

The decision to exploit structured and semi-structured data is based on a key observation, namely that underlying the current unstructured "web of text and pictures" is

---

[1] The Unreasonable Effectiveness of Data Alon Halevy, Peter Norvig, and Fernando Pereira, IEEE Intelligent Systems, March/April 2009, pgs 8-12, http://static.googleusercontent.com/external_content/untrusted_dlcp/research.google.com/en//pubs/archive/35179.pdf.

[2]   http://www.readwriteweb.com/archives/web_of_data_machine_accessible_information.php.

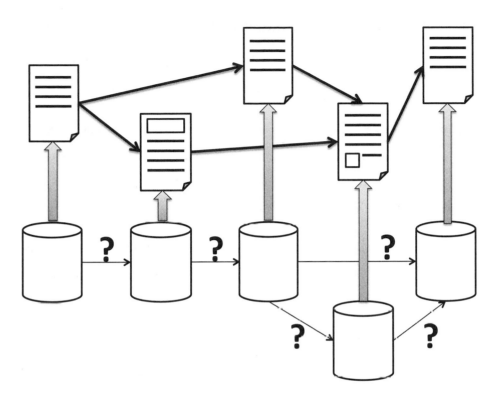

Figure 1.1: Structured and unstructured data on the web

actually a very large amount of structured and semi-structured data. The vast majority of web content is being generated from databases and content management systems containing carefully structured datasets. However, the often rich structure that is available in such datasets is almost completely lost in the process of publishing such structured data as human-readable Hypertext Markup Language (HTML) pages (see figure 1.1). A key insight is that we would have made major strides towards the vision of a more Semantic Web if only we could publish and interlink the underlying structured datasets (instead of just publishing and interlinking the HTML pages after much of the underlying structure has been lost).

1.1.3   Basic Technology for the Semantic Web

The aforementioned three design principles have been translated into actual technology, and much of this book will be devoted to describing just that technology:

1. use *labeled graphs* as the data model for objects and their relations, with objects as nodes in the graph, and the edges in the graph depicting the relations between these objects. The unfortunately named "Resource Descripion Framework" *RDF*[3] is used as the formalism to represent such graphs.

2. use *web identifiers (Uniform Resource Identifiers - URI)* to identify the individual data-items and their relations that appear in the datasets. Again, this is reflected in the design of RDF.

3. use *ontologies* (briefly: hierarchical vocabularies of types and relations) as the data model to formally represent the intended semantics of the data. Formalisms such as *RDF Schema* and *The Web Ontology Language* (OWL) are used for this purpose, again using URIs to represent the types and their properties.

1.1.4   From Data to Knowledge

It is important to realize that in order to really capture the intended semantics of the data, a formalism such as RDF Schema and OWL are not just data-description languages, but are actually lightweight *knowledge representation* languages. They are "logics" that allow the inference of additional information from the explicitly stated information. RDF Schema is a very low expressivity logic that allows some very simple inferences, such as property inheritance over a hierarchy of types and type-inference of domain and range restrictions. Similarly, OWL is somewhat richer (but still relatively lightweight) logic that allows additional inferences such as equality and inequality, number restrictions, existence of objects and others. Such inferences in RDF Schema

---

[3]Perhaps "Rich Data Format" would be a better name.

and OWL give publishers of information the possibility to create a minimal lowerbound of facts that readers must believe about published data. Additionally, OWL gives information publishers the possibility to forbid readers of information to believe certain things about the published data (at least as long as everybody intends to stay consistent with the published ontology).

Together, performing such inferences over these logics amounts to imposing both a lower bound and an upper bound on the intended semantics of the published data. By increasingly refining the ontologies, these lower and upper bounds can be moved arbitrarily close together, thereby pinning down ever more precisely the intended semantics of the data, to the extent required by the use cases at hand.

1.1.5   The Web Architecture of the Semantic Web

A key aspect of the traditional web is the fact that its content is distributed, both in location and in ownership: web pages that link to each other often live on different web servers, and these servers are in different physical locations and owned by different parties. A crucial contributor to the growth of the web is the fact that "anybody can say anything about anything,"[4] or more precisely: anybody can refer to anybody's web page without having to negotiate first about permissions or inquire about the right address or identifier to use. A similar mechanism is at work in the Semantic Web (see figure 1.2): a first party can publish a dataset on the web (left side of the diagram), a second party can independently publish a vocabulary of terms (right side of the diagram), and a third party may decide to annotate the object of the first party with a term published by the second party, without asking for permission from either of them, and in fact without either of these two having to even know about it. It is this decoupling that is the essence of the weblike nature of the Semantic Web.

---

[4] http://www.w3.org/DesignIssues/RDFnot.html.

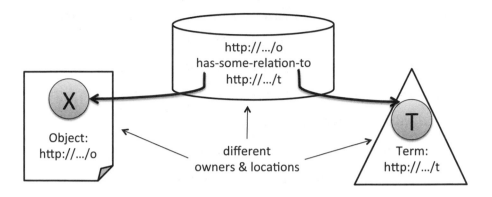

Figure 1.2: Web architecture for linked data

1.1.6   How to Get There from Here

Of course, some significant steps are required in order to make the above vision and architectural principles an implemented reality:

1. We must agree on standard syntax to represent data and metadata.

2. We must have sufficient agreement on the metadata vocabularies in order to share intended semantics of the data.

3. We must publish large volumes of data in the formats of step 1, using the vocabularies of step 2.

Over the past decade (the earliest Semantic Web projects date from the last years of the twentieth century), substantial progress has been made on all three of these steps: the languages RDF, RDF Schema, and OWL (and their variations, such as RDFa, OWL2, etc.) have all acquired the formal support of the World Wide Web Consortium (W3C), elevating them to de facto standards on the web. Many thousands of vocabularies have been published in these formats[5] and convergence among these vocabularies is beginning to occur, both as a result of automated ontology mapping technology

---

[5] http://swoogle.umbc.edu/.

and under the pressure of social and economic demands (e.g., the development of the schema.org vocabulary).[6] And the growth of the Linked Data Cloud[7] has resulted in many billions of objects and their relations becoming available online, using shared syntax and vocabularies.

1.1.7   Where We Are Now

When compared with the situation at the publication of the first edition of this Semantic Web Primer, in 2003, many of the building blocks are now in place. There is rapidly maturing technology to support all phases of deployment of Semantic Web technology, and the number of substantial adoptions, both in commercial and public organizations, is growing rapidly. However, major challenges remain, such as dealing with the ever-increasing scale, lowering the barrier of adoption, and of course fighting that omnipresent bane of information systems: semantic heterogeneity.

1.2   Semantic Web Technologies

1.2.1   Explicit Metadata

Currently, web content is formatted for human readers rather than programs. HTML is the predominant language in which web pages are written (directly or using tools). A portion of a typical web page of a physical therapist might look like this:

```
<h1>Agilitas Physiotherapy Centre</h1>
Welcome to the Agilitas Physiotherapy Centre home page.
Do you feel pain? Have you had an injury? Let our staff
Lisa Davenport, Kelly Townsend (our lovely secretary)
and Steve Matthews take care of your body and soul.
```

---

[6] http://schema.org.
[7] http:/linkeddata.org.

```
<h2>Consultation hours</h2>
Mon 11am - 7pm<br>
Tue 11am - 7pm<br>
Wed 3pm - 7pm<br>
Thu 11am - 7pm<br>
Fri 11am - 3pm<p>
But note that we do not offer consultation
during the weeks of the
<a href=". . .">State of Origin</a> games.
```

For people the information is presented in a satisfactory way, but machines will have problems. Keyword-based searches will identify the words *physiotherapy* and *consultation hours*. And an intelligent agent might even be able to identify the personnel of the center. But it will have trouble distinguishing the therapists from the secretary, and even more trouble finding the exact consultation hours (for which it would have to follow the link to the State of Origin games to find when they take place).

The Semantic Web approach to solving these problems is not the development of superintelligent agents. Instead it proposes to attack the problem from the web page side. If HTML is replaced by more appropriate languages, then web pages can carry their content on their sleeve. In addition to containing formatting information aimed at producing a document for human readers, they could contain information about their content.

A first step in this direction is eXtensible Markup Language (XML), which allows one to define the structure of information on web pages. In our example, there might be information such as:

```
<company>
  <treatmentOffered>Physiotherapy</treatmentOffered>
  <companyName>Agilitas Physiotherapy Centre</companyName>
```

```
<staff>
    <therapist>Lisa Davenport</therapist>
    <therapist>Steve Matthews</therapist>
    <secretary>Kelly Townsend</secretary>
</staff>
</company>
```

This representation is far more easily processable by machines. In particular, it is useful for exchanging information on the web, which is one of the most prominent application areas of XML technology.

However, XML still remains at the syntactic level, as it describes the *structure* of information, but not its *meaning*. The basic language of the Semantic Web is RDF, which is a language for making statements about pieces of information. In our example, such statements include:

Company A offer physiotherapy.

The name of A is "Agitilitas Physiotherapy".

Lisa Davenport is a therapist.

Lisa Davenport works for A.

...

To a human reader, the difference between the XML representation and a list of RDF statements may appear minimal, but they are quite different in nature: XML describes structure while RDF makes statements about pieces of information.[8]

The term *metadata* refers to such information: data about data. Metadata captures part of the *meaning* of data, thus the term *semantic* in Semantic Web.

---

[8]A human reader assigns meaning to the XML representation based on the chosen tag names, but this is not so for machine processors.

1.2.2   Ontologies

The term *ontology* originates from philosophy. In that context, it is used as the name of a subfield of philosophy, namely, the study of the nature of existence (the literal translation of the Greek word $O\nu\tau o\lambda o\gamma i\alpha$), the branch of metaphysics concerned with identifying, in the most general terms, the kinds of things that actually exist, and how to describe them. For example, the observation that the world is made up of specific objects that can be grouped into abstract classes based on shared properties is a typical ontological commitment.

However, in more recent years, *ontology* has become one of the many words hijacked by computer science and given a specific technical meaning that is rather different from the original one. Instead of "ontology" we now speak of "*an* ontology." For our purposes, we will use T. R. Gruber's definition, later refined by R. Studer: *An ontology is an explicit and formal specification of a conceptualization.*

In general, an ontology describes formally a domain of discourse. Typically, an ontology consists of a finite list of terms and the relationships between these terms. The *terms* denote important *concepts* (*classes* of objects) of the domain. For example, in a university setting, staff members, students, courses, lecture theaters, and disciplines are some important concepts.

The *relationships* typically include hierarchies of classes. A hierarchy specifies a class C to be a subclass of another class C' if every object in C is also included in C'. For example, all faculty are staff members. Figure 1.3 shows a hierarchy for the university domain.

Apart from subclass relationships, ontologies may include information such as

- properties (X teaches Y),

- value restrictions (only faculty members may teach courses),

- disjointness statements (faculty and general staff are disjoint),

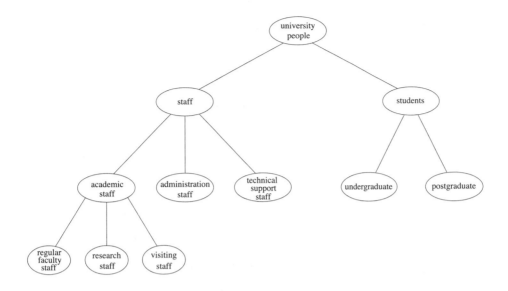

Figure 1.3: A hierarchy

- specifications of logical relationships between objects (every department must include at least ten faculty members).

In the context of the web, ontologies provide *a shared understanding of a domain.* Such a shared understanding is necessary to overcome differences in terminology. One application's zip code may be the same as another application's postcode. Another problem is that two applications may use the same term with different meanings. In university A, a course may refer to a degree (like computer science), while in university B it may mean a single subject (CS 101). Such differences can be overcome by mapping the particular terminology to a shared ontology or by defining direct mappings between the ontologies. In either case, it is easy to see that ontologies support semantic interoperability.

Ontologies are useful for the organization and navigation of websites. Many websites today expose on the left-hand side of the page the top levels of a concept hierarchy of terms. The user may click on one of them to expand the subcategories.

Also, ontologies are useful for improving the accuracy of web searches. The search engines can look for pages that refer to a precise *concept* in an ontology instead of collecting all pages in which certain, generally ambiguous, keywords occur. In this way, differences in terminology between web pages and queries can be overcome.

In addition, web searches can exploit generalization/specialization information. If a query fails to find any relevant documents, the search engine may suggest to the user a more general query. It is even conceivable for the engine to run such queries proactively to reduce the reaction time in case the user adopts a suggestion. Or if too many answers are retrieved, the search engine may suggest to the user some specializations.

In Artificial Intelligence (AI) there is a long tradition of developing and using ontology languages. It is a foundation Semantic Web research can build on. At present, the most important ontology languages for the web are the following:

- RDF Schema is a vocabulary description language for describing properties and classes of RDF resources, with a semantics for generalization hierarchies of such properties and classes. In addition, domain and range of properties may be defined.

- OWL is a richer vocabulary description language for describing properties and classes, such as relations between classes (e.g., disjointness), cardinality (e.g., "exactly one"), equality, richer typing of properties, characteristics of properties (e.g., symmetry), and enumerated classes.

1.2.3   Logic

Logic is the discipline that studies the principles of reasoning; it goes back to Aristotle. In general, logic first offers *formal languages* for expressing knowledge. Second, logic provides us with *well-understood formal semantics*: in most logics, the meaning of sentences is defined without the need to operationalize the knowledge. Often we speak of declarative knowledge: we describe *what* holds without caring about *how* it can be deduced.

And third, automated reasoners can deduce (infer) conclusions from the given knowledge, thus making implicit knowledge explicit. Such reasoners have been studied extensively in AI. Here is an example of an inference. Suppose we know that all professors are faculty members, that all faculty members are staff members, and that Michael is a professor. In predicate logic the information is expressed as follows:

$$prof(X) \rightarrow faculty(X)$$

$$faculty(X) \rightarrow staff(X)$$

$$prof(michael)$$

Then we can deduce the following:

$$faculty(michael)$$

$$staff(michael)$$

$$prof(X) \rightarrow staff(X)$$

Note that this example involves knowledge typically found in ontologies. Thus logic can be used to uncover ontological knowledge that is implicitly given. By doing so, it can also help uncover unexpected relationships and inconsistencies.

But logic is more general than ontologies. It can also be used by intelligent agents for making decisions and selecting courses of action. For example, a shop agent may decide to grant a discount to a customer based on the rule

$$loyalCustomer(X) \rightarrow discount(X, 5\%)$$

where the loyalty of customers is determined from data stored in the corporate database.

Generally there is a trade-off between expressive power and computational efficiency. The more expressive a logic is, the more computationally expensive it becomes to draw conclusions. And drawing certain conclusions may become impossible if non-computability barriers are encountered. Luckily, most knowledge relevant to the Semantic Web seems to be of a relatively restricted form. For example, our previous examples involved *rules* of the form, "If conditions, then conclusion," where conditions and conclusion are simple statements, and only a finite number of objects need to be considered. This subset of logic, called Horn logic, is tractable and supported by efficient reasoning tools.

An important advantage of logic is that it can provide *explanations* for conclusions: the series of inference steps can be retraced. Moreover, AI researchers have developed ways of presenting an explanation in a human-friendly way, by organizing a proof as a natural deduction and by grouping a number of low-level inference steps into metasteps that a person will typically consider a single proof step. Ultimately an explanation will trace an answer back to a given set of facts and the inference rules used.

Explanations are important for the Semantic Web because they increase users' confidence in Semantic Web agents (see the previous physiotherapy example). Tim Berners-Lee speaks of an "Oh yeah?" button that would ask for an explanation.

Explanations will also be necessary for activities between agents. While some agents will be able to draw logical conclusions, others will only have the capability to *validate proofs*, that is, to check whether a claim made by another agent is substantiated. Here is a simple example. Suppose agent 1, representing an online shop, sends a message "You owe me \$80" (not in natural language, of course, but in a formal, machine-processable language) to agent 2, representing a person. Then agent 2 might ask for an explanation, and agent 1 might respond with a sequence of the form

Web log of a purchase over \$80

Proof of delivery (for example, tracking number of UPS)

Rule from the shop's terms and conditions:

$$purchase(X, Item) \land price(Item, Price) \land delivered(Item, X)$$
$$\rightarrow owes(X, Price)$$

Thus facts will typically be traced to some web addresses (the trust of which will be verifiable by agents), and the rules may be a part of a shared commerce ontology or the policy of the online shop.

For logic to be useful on the web it must be usable in conjunction with other data, and it must be machine-processable as well. Therefore, there is ongoing work on representing logical knowledge and proofs in web languages. Initial approaches work at the level of XML, but in the future rules and proofs will need to be represented at the level of RDF and ontology languages.

1.2.4   The Semantic Web versus Artificial Intelligence

As we have said, most of the technologies needed for the realization of the Semantic Web build on work in the area of artificial intelligence. Given that AI has a long history, not always commercially successful, one might worry that, in the worst case, the Semantic Web will repeat AI's errors: big promises that raise too high expectations, which turn out not to be fulfilled (at least not in the promised time frame).

This worry is unjustified. The realization of the Semantic Web vision does not rely on human-level intelligence; in fact, as we have tried to explain, the challenges are approached in a different way. The full problem of AI is a deep scientific one, perhaps comparable to the central problems of physics (explain the physical world) or biology (explain the living world). So seen, the difficulties in achieving human-level Artificial Intelligence within ten or twenty years, as promised at some points in the past, should not have come as a surprise.

But on the Semantic Web partial solutions work. Even if an intelligent agent is not able to come to all conclusions that a human user might, the agent will still contribute to a web much superior to the current one. This brings us to another difference. If the ultimate goal of AI is to build an intelligent agent exhibiting human-level intelligence (and higher), the goal of the Semantic Web is to assist human users in their day-to-day online activities.

It is clear that the Semantic Web makes extensive use of current AI technology and that advances in that technology will lead to a better Semantic Web. But there is no need to wait until AI reaches a higher level of achievement; current AI technology is already sufficient to go a long way toward realizing the Semantic Web vision.

1.3   A Layered Approach

The development of the Semantic Web proceeds in steps, each step building a *layer* on top of another. The pragmatic justification for this approach is that it is easier to achieve consensus on small steps, whereas it is much harder to get everyone on board if too much is attempted. Usually there are several research groups moving in different directions; this competition of ideas is a major driving force for scientific progress. However, from an engineering perspective there is a need to standardize. So, if most researchers agree on certain issues and disagree on others, it makes sense to fix the points of agreement. This way, even if the more ambitious research efforts should fail, there will be at least partial positive outcomes.

Once a standard has been established, many more groups and companies will adopt it instead of waiting to see which of the alternative research lines will be successful in the end. The nature of the Semantic Web is such that companies and single users must build tools, add content, and use that content. We cannot wait until the full Semantic Web vision materializes — it may take another ten years for it to be realized to its full extent (as envisioned today, of course).

In building one layer of the Semantic Web on top of another, two principles should be followed:

- Downward compatibility. Agents fully aware of a layer should also be able to interpret and use information written at lower levels. For example, agents aware of the semantics of OWL can take full advantage of information written in RDF and RDF Schema.

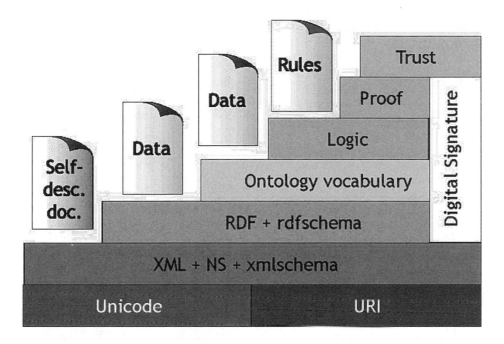

Figure 1.4: A layered approach to the Semantic Web

- Upward partial understanding. The design should be such that agents fully aware of a layer should be able to take at least partial advantage of information at higher levels. For example, an agent aware only of the RDF and RDF Schema semantics might interpret knowledge written in OWL partly, by disregarding those elements that go beyond RDF and RDF Schema. Of course, there is no requirement for all tools to provide this functionality; the point is that this option should be enabled.

While these ideas are theoretically appealing and have been used as guiding principles for the development of the Semantic Web, their realization in practice has turned out to be difficult, and some compromises have needed to be made. This will become clear in chapter 4, where the layering of RDF and OWL is discussed.

Figure 1.4 shows the "layer cake" of the Semantic Web, which describes the main layers of the Semantic Web design and vision. At the bottom we find *XML*, a language that lets one write structured web documents with a user-defined vocabulary. XML is particularly suitable for sending documents across the web. In addition, URIs used in XML can be grouped by their *namespace*, signified by NS in the diagram.

RDF is a basic data model, like the entity-relationship model, for writing simple statements about web objects (resources). The RDF data model does not rely on XML, but RDF has an XML-based syntax. Therefore, in figure 1.4, it is located on top of the XML layer.

RDF Schema provides modeling primitives for organizing web objects into hierarchies. Key primitives are classes and properties, subclass and subproperty relationships, and domain and range restrictions. RDF Schema is based on RDF.

RDF Schema can be viewed as a primitive language for writing ontologies. But there is a need for more powerful *ontology languages* that expand RDF Schema and allow the representations of more complex relationships between web objects. The *Logic* layer is used to enhance the ontology language further and to allow the writing of application-specific declarative knowledge.

The *Proof layer* involves the actual deductive process as well as the representation of proofs in web languages (from lower levels) and proof validation.

Finally, the *Trust layer* will emerge through the use of *digital signatures* and other kinds of knowledge, based on recommendations by trusted agents or on rating and certification agencies and consumer bodies. Sometimes "Web of Trust" is used to indicate that trust will be organized in the same distributed and chaotic way as the web itself. Being located at the top of the pyramid, trust is a high-level and crucial concept: the web will only achieve its full potential when users have trust in its operations (security) and in the quality of information provided.

This classical layer cake was a major driver in the agenda of the Semantic Web, but is now quite outdated. In particular, a number of alternatives for the ontology vocabulary layer have emerged. In addition, rule languages have been defined on top of RDF, bypassing the ontology vocabulary layer; this is particularly true in the recent shift from rich semantic structures to the processing of huge amounts of (semantic) data. Thus, this layer cake is included here for illustration purposes, as a means of presenting a historic view of the Semantic Web.

1.4   Book Overview

In this book we concentrate on the Semantic Web technologies that have reached a reasonable degree of maturity.

In chapter 2 we discuss RDF and RDF Schema. RDF is a language in which we can express statements about objects (resources); it is a standard data model for machine-processable semantics. RDF Schema offers a number of modeling primitives for organizing RDF vocabularies in typed hierarchies.

Chapter 3 is devoted to the query language SPARQL that plays the same role in the RDF world as SQL in the relational world.

Chapter 4 discusses OWL2, the current revision of OWL, a web ontology language. It offers more modeling primitives than RDF Schema, and it has a clean, formal semantics.

Chapter 5 is devoted to rules in the framework of the Semantic Web. While rules on the semantic web have not yet reached the same level of community agreement as RDF, SPARQL, or OWL, the principles to be adopted are quite clear, so it makes sense to present them here.

Chapter 6 discusses several application domains and explains the benefits that they will draw from the materialization of the Semantic Web vision.

Chapter 7 describes various key issues regarding the development of ontology-based systems for the web.

Finally, chapter 8 discusses briefly a few issues that are currently under debate in the Semantic Web community.

1.5 Summary

- The Semantic Web is an initiative that aims at improving the current state of the World Wide Web.

- The key idea is the use of machine-processable web information.

- Key technologies include data publication with explicit metadata, ontologies, logic, and inferencing.

- The development of the Semantic Web proceeds in layers.

Suggested Reading

An excellent introductory article on the Semantic Web vision is

- T. Berners-Lee, J. Hendler, and O. Lassila. The Semantic Web. *Scientific American* 284 (May 2001): 34–43.

An inspirational book about the history (and the future) of the web is

- T. Berners-Lee, with M. Fischetti. *Weaving the Web*. San Francisco: Harper, 1999.

A number of websites maintain up-to-date information about the Semantic Web and related topics:

- www.semanticweb.org/.

- www.w3.org/2001/sw/.

There is a good selection of research papers providing technical information on issues relating to the Semantic Web:

- J. Domingue, D. Fensel, and J. Hendler. *Handbook of Semantic Web Technologies*. Springer, 2011.

Key venues where the most important recent advances in the ideas, technologies, and applications of the Semantic Web are published are:

- The conference series of the *International Semantic Web Conference*. See http://www.semanticweb.org/.

- The conference series of the *Extended (European) Semantic Web Conference*. See http://www.eswc.org/.

- Journal   of   Web   Semantics.   http://www.journals.elsevier.com/journal-of-web-semantics/.

A number of books dedicated to the Semantic Web have appeared in recent years. Among them

- D. Allemang and J. Hendler. *Semantic Web for the Working Ontologist: Effective Modeling in RDFS and OWL*. New York, NY.: Morgan Kaufmann, 2008.

focuses on ontological modeling issues, while

- P. Hitzler, M. Kroetzsch, and S. Rudolph. *Foundations of Semantic Web Technologies*. Boca Raton, FL.: Chapman and Hall, 2009.

focuses on the logical foundations.

Chapter 2

Describing Web Resources: RDF

2.1 Introduction

The success of the WWW has shown the power of having standard mechanisms to exchange and communicate information. HTML is the standard language in which web pages are written. It allows anyone to publish a document and have confidence that this document will be rendered correctly by any web browser.

There are three components that HTML and any exchange language has: a syntax, a data model, and a semantics. A syntax tells us how to write data down. A data model tells us the structure or organization of the data. A semantics tells us how to interpret that data. We can illustrate each of these components with a snippet of HTML:

```
<html>
    <head>
        <title>Apartments for Rent</title>
        </head>
```

23

```
<body>
    <ol>
            <li> Studio apartment on Florida Ave.
            <li> 3 bedroom Apartment on Baron Way
        </ol>
    </body>
</html>
```

The syntax of HTML is text with tags (e.g. <title>) written using angle brackets. The data model of HTML, known as the Document Object Model, defines the organization of these elements defined by tags into a hierarchical tree structure. For example, <head> should come before <body> and <li> elements should appear within <ol> elements. Finally, the semantics of HTML tell us how the browser should interpret the web page. For example, the browser should render the content of the web page's body within the browser window and <ol> elements should be displayed as an ordered list. The syntax, data model, and semantics are all defined within the HTML standard.

HTML is designed to communicate information about the structure of documents for human consumption. For the Semantic Web, we need something richer. We need a data model that can be used by multiple applications, not just for describing documents for people but for describing application-specific information. This data model needs to be *domain independent* so that applications ranging from real estate to social networks can leverage it. In addition to a flexible data model, we also need a mechanism to assign semantics to the information represented using this data model. It should allow users to describe how an application should interpret "friend" in a social network description and "city" in a geographical description. Finally, like HTML, we need a way to write down all this information – a syntax.

RDF (Resource Description Framework) provides just such a flexible domain independent data model. Its basic building block is an entity-attribute-value triple, called a statement. Examples of statements we can represent using such a model include "The Baron Way Apartment is an Apartment," "The Baron Way Apartment is part of The Baron Way Building," and "The Baron Way Building is located in Amsterdam." Because RDF is not particular to any domain or use, it is necessary for users to define the terminology they use within these statements. To do this, they make use of RDF Schema (RDFS). RDFS allows users to precisely define how their *vocabulary* (i.e. their terminology) should be interpreted.

Combined, these technologies define the components of a standard language for exchanging arbitrary data between machines:

- RDF – data model

- RDFS – semantics

- Turtle / RDFa/ RDF-XML – syntax

While RDF is primarily the data model within this language, it is often used as the name for the whole of it (a sin we commit ourselves within this book).

Chapter Overview

- Section 2.2 describes RDF.

- The various syntaxes used for RDF are presented in section 2.3.

- The basics of RDF Schema are introduced in section 2.4 and the complete language is presented in section 2.5 and section 2.6.

- The formal meaning of RDFS is given from two perspectives in sections 2.7 and 2.8.

2.2   RDF: Data Model

The fundamental concepts of RDF are resources, properties, statements, and graphs.

2.2.1   Resources

We can think of a resource as an object, a "thing" we want to talk about. Resources may be authors, apartments, tennis players, places, people, hotels, search queries, and so on. Every resource has a URI. A URI can be a URL (Uniform Resource Locator, or web address) or another kind of unique identifier. URI schemes have been defined not only for web locations but also for telephone numbers, ISBN numbers, and geographic locations. URIs provide a mechanism to unambiguously identify the "thing" we want to talk about. Thus, if referring to a swimming pool, we can use a URI assigned to swimming pools and not have it be confused with billiards (pool) or a group of people (the pool of programmers). This is known as the homonym problem.

The use of a URI does not necessarily enable *access* to a resource. However, using dereferencable URLs for resource identifiers is considered good practice. It enables users to either retrieve a resource itself (in the case of an image) or a further description of that resource (in case of a person). This practice is assumed throughout the book. The use of URIs is one of the key design decisions behind RDF. It allows for a global, worldwide unique naming scheme. The use of such a scheme greatly reduces the homonym problem that has plagued distributed data representation until now.

2.2.2   Properties

Properties are a special kind of resource; they describe relations between other resources – for example, "friend of," "written by," and "located in." Like all resources, properties are identified by URIs. We can also dereference property URLs to find their descriptions.

2.2.3   Statements

Statements assert the properties of resources. A statement is an entity-attribute-value triple, consisting of a resource, a property, and a value. The value can either be a

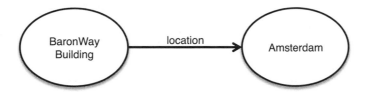

Figure 2.1: An RDF statement represented graphically

resource or a *literal*. Literals are atomic values – for example, numbers, strings, or dates. We often use the word subject to refer to the entity in a statement and object to refer to its value.

Take an example statement "Baron Way Building is located in Amsterdam." We can write this as:

```
<http://www.semanticwebprimer.org/ontology/apartments.ttl#BaronWayBuilding>
<http://dbpedia.org/ontology/location>
<http://dbpedia.org/resource/Amsterdam>.
```

Notice how we used URLs to identify the things we are referring to in our statement.

2.2.4 Graphs

We can also write this same statement down graphically. Note that we leave off the URIs in the picture for readability.

In figure 2.1, labeled nodes are connected by labeled arcs. The arcs are directed from the subject of the statement to the object of the statement, with the label on the arc to the statement's property. The labels on the nodes are the identifiers of the subject and object. The object of a statement can be the subject of another statement. For example, we can say that "Amsterdam is a city." We can see this graphically in figure 2.2.

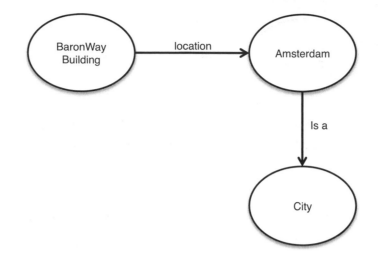

Figure 2.2: An RDF graph

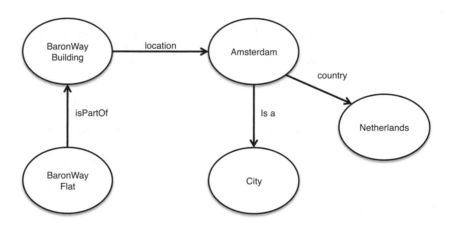

Figure 2.3: An expanded RDF graph

This graphical representation highlights the notion that RDF is a graph-centric data model. Indeed, RDF resembles what is termed a semantic net in the Artificial Intelligence community. We can continue to expand the graph with information about the Baron Way Building. Figure 2.3 shows an expanded version of our RDF graph.

Importantly, this graph can be created in a *distributed* fashion by multiple different participants just by using the same URLs. This allows us to create a *Web of Data* allowing for knowledge to be reused; for example, if we find RDF on the web describing Amsterdam, we can reuse that information just by using that URL. Indeed, there is a set of best practices, called the *Linked Data principles*,[1] that encourage us to reuse and make available information to help create this global graph.

1. Use URIs as names for things.

2. Use HTTP URIs so that people can look up those names.

3. When someone looks up a URI, provide useful information, using the standards (RDF).

4. Include links to other URIs so that they can discover more things.

While the RDF data model does not require that we follow these principles, by doing so we can take advantage of the contributed knowledge of others. Notice how we have reused this information from DBpedia.org in our examples. You can follow these URLs to find out more information about the referred to concepts.

2.2.5   Pointing to Statements and Graphs

Sometimes it is useful to be able to point to particular statements and parts of graphs, such as when assigning a degree of belief in a statement or identifying where a statement has come from. For example, we may want to say that the statement about the location of the Baron Way Building was created by a person, Frank. RDF provides two mechanisms for doing so.

One is called *reification*. The key idea behind reification is to introduce an auxiliary object, say, *LocationStatement*, and relate it to each of the three parts of the original

---

[1] http://www.w3.org/DesignIssues/LinkedData.html.

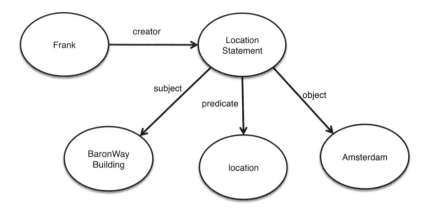

Figure 2.4: An example of reification

statement through the properties *subject*, *predicate*, and *object*. In the preceding example the subject of *LocationStatement* would be *BaronWayBuilding*, the predicate would be *location*, and the object *Amsterdam*. We can then refer to the statement in the subject of another triple that defines the creator. Figure 2.4 depicts the resulting graph. Again, the full URIs are not shown for presentation purposes.

This rather cumbersome approach is necessary because there are only triples in RDF; therefore we cannot add an identifier directly to a triple (then it would be a quadruple). Because of the overhead of reification, in newer versions of the RDF standard, the notion of named graphs was introduced. Here, an explicit identifier (again a URL) is given to a statement or set of statements. This identifier can then be referred to in normal triples. This is a more straightforward mechanism for identifying statements as well as graphs. Simply put, a named graph allows one to circle a set of RDF statements and provide these statement an identifier. Section 2.3.1.3 provides an example of the above reified statement using named graphs.

2.2.6   Dealing with Richer Predicates

We can think of a triple (x, P, y) as a logical formula $P(x, y)$, where the binary predicate P relates the object x to the object y. In fact, *RDF offers only binary predicates (properties).* However, in some cases we may need predicates that have more than two arguments. Luckily, such predicates can be simulated by a number of binary predicates. We illustrate this technique for a predicate *broker* with three arguments. The intuitive meaning of *broker(X, Y, Z)* is

> *X* is the broker in a home sale between seller *Y* and purchaser *Z*.

We now introduce a new auxiliary resource *home-sale* and the binary predicates *broker*, *seller*, and *purchaser*. Then we can represent *broker(X, Y, Z)* as follows:

> *broker(home-sale, X)*
>
> *seller(home-sale, Y)*
>
> *purchaser(home-sale, Z)*

While the predicate with three arguments is more succinct to write, the use of binary predicates does simplify the overall data model.

2.3   RDF Syntaxes

We have already seen one syntax for RDF, namely, a graphical syntax. This syntax is, however, neither machine interpretable nor standardized. Here, we introduce a standard machine interpretable syntax called *Turtle*, and briefly discuss some alternatives.

2.3.1   Turtle

Terse RDF Triple Language (Turtle) is a text-based syntax for RDF. The file extension used for Turtle text files is ".ttl". We have already seen how to write a statement in Turtle earlier. Here's an example:

<http://www.semanticwebprimer.org/ontology/apartments.ttl#BaronWayBuilding>
<http://dbpedia.org/ontology/location>
<http://dbpedia.org/resource/Amsterdam>.

URLs are enclosed in angle brackets. The subject, property, and object of a statement appear in order, followed by a period. Indeed, we can write a whole RDF graph just using this approach.

<http://www.semanticwebprimer.org/ontology/apartments.ttl#>
    <http://www.semanticwebprimer.org/ontology/apartments.ttl#isPartOf>
    <http://www.semanticwebprimer.org/ontology/apartments.ttl#BaronWayBuilding>.
<http://www.semanticwebprimer.org/ontology/apartments.ttl#BaronWayBuilding>
    <http://dbpedia.org/ontology/location>
    <http://dbpedia.org/resource/Amsterdam>.

2.3.1.1   Literals

So far we have defined statements that link together resources. As discussed previously, we can also include literals, that is, atomic values within RDF. In Turtle, we write this down by simply enclosing the value in quotes and appending it with the *data type* of the value. A data type tells us whether we should interpret a value as string, a date, integer or some other type. Data types are again expressed as URLs. It is recommend practice to use the data types defined by XML Schema. When using these data types the values must conform to the XML Schema definition. If no data type is specified after a literal, it is assumed to be a string. Here are some common data types and how they look in Turtle:

string - ''Baron Way''
integers - ''1''^^<http://www.w3.org/2001/XMLSchema#integer>
decimals - ''1.23'' <http://www.w3.org/2001/XMLSchema#decimal>
dates - ''1982-08-30''^^<http://www.w3.org/2001/XMLSchema#date>

time - "11:24:00"^^<http://www.w3.org/2001/XMLSchema#time>

date with a time -

 "1982-08-30T11:24:00"^^<http://www.w3.org/2001/XMLSchema#dateTime>

Suppose that we want to add to our graph that the Baron Way Apartment has three bedrooms. We would add the following statement in Turtle to our graph.

<http://www.semanticwebprimer.org/ontology/apartments.ttl#BaronWayApartment>

<http://www.semanticwebprimer.org/ontology/apartments.ttl#hasNumberOfBedrooms>

"3"^^<http://www.w3.org/2001/XMLSchema#integer>.

<http://www.semanticwebprimer.org/ontology/apartments.ttl#BaronWayApartment>

<http://www.semanticwebprimer.org/ontology/apartments.ttl#isPartOf>

<http://www.semanticwebprimer.org/ontology/apartments.ttl#BaronWayBuilding>.

<http://www.semanticwebprimer.org/ontology/apartments.ttl#BaronWayBuilding>

<http://dbpedia.org/ontology/location>

<http://dbpedia.org/resource/Amsterdam>.

The examples above are rather unwieldy. To make things clearer, Turtle provides a number of constructs to make it easier to write things down.

2.3.1.2 Abbreviations

Often when we define vocabularies, we do so at the same URI. In our example, the resources Baron Way Apartment and Baron Way Building are both defined at the URL http://www.semanticwebprimer.org/ontology/apartments.ttl. This URL defines what is termed the *namespace* of those resources. Turtle takes advantage of this convention to allow URLs to be abbreviated. It introduces the @prefix syntax to define short stand-ins for particular namespaces. For example, we can say that swp should be the stand-in for http://www.semanticwebprimer.org/ontology/apartments.ttl. Such a stand-in is termed a *qualified name*. Below is a rewrite of our example using prefixes.

@prefix swp: <http://www.semanticwebprimer.org/ontology/apartments.ttl#>.

@prefix dbpedia: <http://dbpedia.org/resource/>.

@prefix dbpedia-owl: <http://dbpedia.org/ontology/>.

@prefix xsd: <http://www.w3.org/2001/XMLSchema#>.

swp:BaronWayApartment swp:hasNumberOfBedrooms "3"^^<xsd:integer>.

swp:BaronWayApartment swp:isPartOf swp:BaronWayBuilding.

swp:BaronWayBuilding dbpedia-owl:location dbpedia:Amsterdam.

Note that the angle brackets are dropped from around resources that are referred to using a qualified name. Secondly, we can mix and match regular URLs with these qualified names.

Turtle also allows us to not repeat particular subjects when they are used repeatedly. In the example above, swp:BaronWayApartment is used as the subject of two triples. This can be written more compactly by using a semicolon at the end of a statement. For example:

@prefix swp: <http://www.semanticwebprimer.org/ontology/apartments.ttl#>.

@prefix dbpedia: <http://dbpedia.org/resource/>.

@prefix dbpedia-owl: <http://dbpedia.org/ontology/>.

@prefix xsd: <http://www.w3.org/2001/XMLSchema#>.

swp:BaronWayApartment swp:hasNumberOfBedrooms "3"^^<xsd:integer>;
                                        swp:isPartOf swp:BaronWayBuilding.

swp:BaronWayBuilding dbpedia-owl:location dbpedia:Amsterdam.

If both a subject and predicate are used repeatedly, we can use a comma at the end of a statement. For instance, if we want to extend our example to say that Baron Way Building is not only located in Amsterdam but also in the Netherlands, we can write the following Turtle:

@prefix swp: <http://www.semanticwebprimer.org/ontology/apartments.ttl#>.

@prefix dbpedia: <http://dbpedia.org/resource/>.

@prefix dbpedia-owl: <http://dbpedia.org/ontology/>.

@prefix xsd: <http://www.w3.org/2001/XMLSchema#>.

swp:BaronWayApartment swp:hasNumberOfBedrooms "3"^^<xsd:integer>;

swp:isPartOf swp:BaronWayBuilding.

swp:BaronWayBuilding dbpedia-owl:location dbpedia:Amsterdam,

                                                        dbpedia:Netherlands.

Finally, Turtle also allows us to abbreviate common data types. For example, numbers can be written without quotes. If they contain a decimal (e.g. 14.3), they are interpreted as decimals. If they do not contain a decimal (e.g. 1), they are interpreted as integers. This shortens our example some more:

@prefix swp: <http://www.semanticwebprimer.org/ontology/apartments.ttl#>.

@prefix dbpedia: <http://dbpedia.org/resource/>.

@prefix dbpedia-owl: <http://dbpedia.org/ontology/>.

swp:BaronWayApartment swp:hasNumberOfBedrooms 3;

                          swp:isPartOf swp:BaronWayBuilding.

swp:BaronWayBuilding dbpedia-owl:location dbpedia:Amsterdam,

               dbpedia:Netherlands.

2.3.1.3   Named Graphs

We discussed previously the ability to point to a set of statements together. Trig is an extension to Turtle that allows us to express such a notion. For example, we might want to say that our statements about the Baron Way Apartment were created by a person,

Frank, identified by the URL http://www.cs.vu.nl/~frankh. We do this by putting brackets around the set of statements we want and assigning that set of statements a URL. Let's look at an example:

```
@prefix swp: <http://www.semanticwebprimer.org/ontology/apartments.ttl#>.
@prefix dbpedia: <http://dbpedia.org/resource/>.
@prefix dbpedia-owl: <http://dbpedia.org/ontology/>.
@prefix dc: <http://purl.org/dc/terms/>.


{
    <http://www.semanticwebprimer.org/ontology/apartments.ttl#>
    dc:creator <http://www.cs.vu.nl/ frankh>
}


<http://www.semanticwebprimer.org/ontology/apartments.ttl#>
{
    swp:BaronWayApartment swp:hasNumberOfBedrooms 3;
        swp:isPartOf swp:BaronWayBuilding.
    swp:BaronWayBuilding dbpedia-owl:location dbpedia:Amsterdam,
        dbpedia:Netherlands.
}
```

In this approach, statements that are not part of a particular graph go in a set of brackets without a URL in front. This is called the default graph.

2.3.2   Other Syntaxes

Besides Turtle, there are a number of other syntaxes that we can use to write down RDF. Among them are two other standard syntaxes: RDF/XML and RDFa.

2.3.2.1   RDF/XML

RDF/XML is an encoding of RDF in the XML language. This allows RDF to be used with existing XML processing tools. Originally, RDF/XML was the only standard syntax for RDF. However, Turtle was adopted as an additional standard as it is often easier to read. Below is RDF/XML. Subjects are denoted by the rdf:about within an rdf:Description element (enclosed in brackets). Predicates and objects related to that subject are enclosed in the rdf:Description element. Namespaces can be used through the XML namespaces (xmlns:) construct. All RDF/XML should be enclosed in an element rdf:RDF.

```
<?xml version="1.0" encoding="utf-8"?>
<rdf:RDF xmlns:dbpedia-owl="http://dbpedia.org/ontology/"
  xmlns:dbpedia="http://dbpedia.org/resource/"
  xmlns:rdf="http://www.w3.org/1999/02/22-rdf-syntax-ns#"
  xmlns:swp="http://www.semanticwebprimer.org/ontology/apartments.ttl#">
  <rdf:Description
  rdf:about="http://www.semanticwebprimer.org/ontology/apartments.ttl#BaronWayApartment">
    <swp:hasNumberOfBedrooms
        rdf:datatype="http://www.w3.org/2001/XMLSchema#integer">
            3
        </swp:hasNumberOfBedrooms>
  </rdf:Description>
  <rdf:Description
  rdf:about="http://www.semanticwebprimer.org/ontology/apartments.ttl#BaronWayApartment">
    <swp:isPartOf
      rdf:resource="http://www.semanticwebprimer.org/ontology/apartments.ttl#BaronWayBuilding"/>
  </rdf:Description>
  <rdf:Description
  rdf:about="http://www.semanticwebprimer.org/ontology/apartments.ttl#BaronWayBuilding">
    <dbpedia-owl:location
```

```
       rdf:resource="http://dbpedia.org/resource/Amsterdam"/>
 </rdf:Description>
 <rdf:Description
  rdf:about="http://www.semanticwebprimer.org/ontology/apartments.ttl#BaronWayBuilding">
   <dbpedia-owl:location
     rdf:resource="http://dbpedia.org/resource/Netherlands"/>
 </rdf:Description>
</rdf:RDF>
```

2.3.2.2 RDFa

One use case of RDF is to describe or mark up the content of HTML web pages. In order to make it easier, a syntax RDFa was introduced to help with that use case. RDFa embeds RDF within the attributes of HTML tags. We'll use an example of advertisement for the Baron Way Apartment.

```
<html>
<body>
<H1> Baron Way Apartment for Sale</H1>
The Baron Way Apartment has three bedrooms and is located in the fam-
ily friendly Baron Way Building. The Apartment is located in the north of Amsterdam.
</body>
</html>
```

This page does not contain any machine readable description. We can mark up the page using RDFa as follows:

```
<html xmlns:dbpedia="http://dbpedia.org/resource/"
     xmlns:dbpediaowl="http://dbpedia.org/ontology/"
     xmlns:swp="http://www.semanticwebprimer.org/ontology/apartments.ttl#"
     xmlns:geo="http://www.geonames.org/ontology#">
<body>
```

```
<H1> Baron Way Flat for Sale</H1>

<div about="[swp:BaronWayFlat]">
```

The Baron Way Flat has <span property="swp:hasNumberOfBedrooms">3</span> bedrooms and is located in the family friendly <span rel="swp:isPartOf" resource="[swp:BaronWayBuilding]">Baron Way Building</span>

```
<div about="[swp:BaronWayBuilding]">
```

The building is located in the north of Amsterdam.
```
  <span rel="dbpediaowl:location" resource="[dbpedia:Amsterdam]"></span>
  <span rel="dbpediaowl:location" resource="[dbpedia:Netherlands]"></span>
</div>

</div>
</body>
</html>
```

This markup will produce the same RDF expressed above in Turtle. Since the RDF is encoded in tags such as spans, paragraphs, and links, the RDF will not be rendered by browsers when displaying the HTML page. Similar to RDF/XML, namespaces are encoded using the xmlns declaration. In some cases, we must use brackets to inform the parser that we are using prefixes. Subjects are identified by the about attribute. Properties are identified by either a rel or property attribute. Rel attributes are used when the object of the statement is a resource whereas a property attribute is used when the object of a statement is a literal. Properties are associated with subjects through the use of the hierarchal structure of HTML.

Each syntax for RDF presented above is useful for different situations. However, it is important to realize that even though different syntaxes may be used, they all share the same underlying data model and semantics. Thus far we have discussed how to write down statements about things identified by URLs. But what do those statements mean? How should a computer go about interpreting the statements made? These questions are discussed in the next section where we introduce a schema language for RDF.

2.4   RDFS: Adding Semantics

RDF is a universal language that lets users describe resources using their own vocabularies. RDF does not make assumptions about any particular application domain, nor does it define the semantics of any domain. In order to specify these semantics, a developer or user of RDF needs to define what those vocabularies mean in terms of a set of basic domain independent structures defined by RDF Schema.

2.4.1   Classes and Properties

How do we describe a particular domain? Let us consider our domain of apartment rentals. First we have to specify the "things" we want to talk about. Here we make a first, fundamental distinction. On one hand, we want to talk about particular apartments, such as the Baron Way Apartment, and particular locations, such as Amsterdam; we have already done so in RDF.

But we also want to talk about apartments, buildings, countries, cities, and so on. What is the difference? In the first case we talk about *individual objects* (resources), and in the second we talk about *classes* that define types of objects.

A class can be thought of as a set of elements. Individual objects that belong to a class are referred to as *instances* of that class. RDF provides us a way to define the relationship between instances and classes using a special property rdf:type.

An important use of classes is to impose restrictions on what can be stated in an RDF document using the schema. In programming languages, *typing* is used to prevent nonsense from being written (such as $A + 1$, where A is an array; we lay down that the arguments of $+$ must be numbers). The same is needed in RDF. After all, we would like to disallow statements such as:

Baron Way Apartment rents Jeff Meyer

Amsterdam has number of bedrooms 3

The first statement is nonsensical because buildings do not rent people. This imposes a restriction on the values of the property "rents." In mathematical terms, we restrict the *range* of the property.

The second statement is nonsensical because cities do not have bedrooms. This imposes a restriction on the objects to which the property can be applied. In mathematical terms, we restrict the *domain* of the property.

2.4.2 Class Hierarchies and Inheritance

Once we have classes, we would also like to establish relationships between them. For example, suppose that we have classes for

unit

residential unit   commercial unit

house & apartment   office

These classes are not unrelated to each other. For example, every residential unit is a unit. We say that "residential unit" is a *subclass* of "unit," or equivalently, that "unit" is a *superclass* of "residential unit." The subclass relationship defines a hierarchy of classes, as shown in figure 2.5. In general, A is a subclass of B if every instance of A is also an instance of B. There is no requirement in RDF Schema that the classes together form a strict hierarchy. In other words, a subclass graph as in figure 2.5 need not be a tree. A class may have multiple superclasses. If a class A is a subclass of both B_1 and B_2, this simply means that every instance of A is both an instance of B_1 and an instance of B_2.

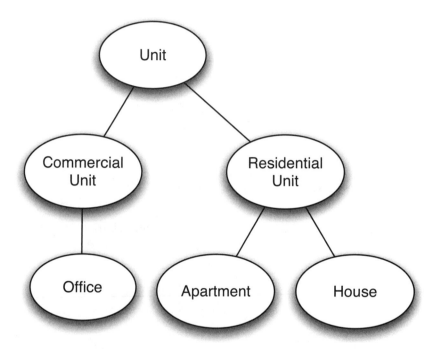

Figure 2.5: A hierarchy of classes

A hierarchical organization of classes has a very important practical significance, which we outline now. Consider the range restriction

People can only rent residential units.

Suppose Baron Way Apartment is defined as an apartment. Then, according to the preceding restriction, it does not qualify as a Residential Unit because there is no statement specifying that the Baron Way Apartment is also a residential unit. It would be counterintuitive to overcome this difficulty by adding that statement to our description. Instead we would like the Baron Way Apartment to *inherit* the ability to be rented from the class of residential units. Exactly this is done in RDF Schema.

By doing so, RDF Schema *fixes the semantics* of "is a subclass of." Now it is not up to an application to interpret "is a subclass of;" instead its intended meaning must be used by all RDF processing software. By making such semantic definitions, RDFS is a (still limited) language for defining the semantics of particular domains. Stated another way, RDF Schema is a primitive *ontology language*.

Classes, inheritance, and properties are, of course, known in other fields of computing – for example, in object-oriented programming. But while there are many similarities, there are differences, too. In object-oriented programming, an object class defines the properties that apply to it. To add new properties to a class means to modify the class.

However, in RDFS, properties are defined globally. That is, they are not encapsulated as attributes in class definitions. It is possible to define new properties that apply to an existing class without changing that class.

On one hand, this is a powerful mechanism with far-reaching consequences: we may use classes defined by others and adapt them to our requirements through new properties. On the other hand, this handling of properties deviates from the standard approach that has emerged in the area of modeling and object-oriented programming. It is another idiosyncratic feature of RDF/RDFS.

2.4.3   Property Hierarchies

We saw that hierarchical relationships between classes can be defined. The same can be done for properties. For example, "rents" is a *subproperty* of "resides at." If a person p rents a residential unit r, then p also resides at r. The converse is not necessarily true. For example, p may be a child living with a family and not paying rent or a person may be just visiting.

In general, if some property P is a subproperty of Q if $Q(x, y)$ whenever $P(x, y)$.

2.4.4   RDF versus RDFS Layers

As a final point, we illustrate the different layers involved in RDF and RDFS using a simple example. Consider the RDF statement

Jeff Meyer rents the Baron Way Apartment.

The schema for this statement may contain classes such as person, apartments, houses, units, and properties such as rents, resides at, or address. Figure 2.6 illustrates the layers of RDF and RDF Schema for this example. In this figure, blocks are properties, bubbles above the dashed line are classes, and bubbles below the dashed line are instances.

The schema in figure 2.6 is itself written in a formal language, RDF Schema, that can express its ingredients: subClassOf, Class, Property, subPropertyOf, Resource, and so on. Next we describe the language of RDF Schema in more detail.

2.5   RDF Schema: The Language

RDF Schema provides modeling primitives for expressing the information described in section 2.5. One decision that must be made is what formal language to use. It should not be surprising that RDF itself will be used: the modeling primitives of RDF Schema are defined using resources and properties. This choice can be justified by looking

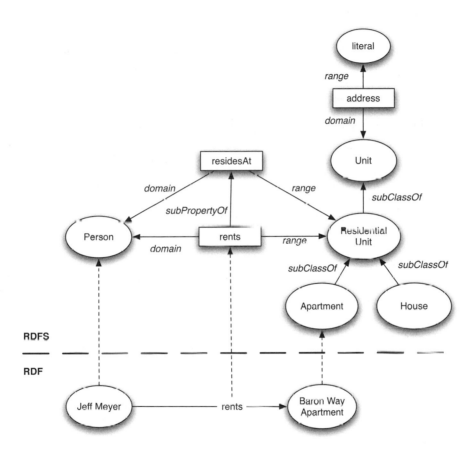

Figure 2.6: RDF and RDFS layers

at figure 2.6. We presented this figure as displaying a class/property hierarchy plus instances, but it is, of course, itself simply a labeled graph that can be encoded in RDF. Remember that RDF allows one to express any statement about any resource, and that anything with a URI can be a resource. So, if we wish to say that the class "apartment" is a subclass of "residential unit," we may.

1. Define the required resources for apartment, residential unit, and subClassOf;

2. define subClassOf to be a property;

3. write the triple (apartment subClassOf residential unit).

All these steps are within the capabilities of RDF. So, an RDFS document is just an RDF document, and we use one of the standard syntaxes for RDF.

Now we define the modeling primitives of RDF Schema.

2.5.1   Core Classes

The core classes are

rdfs:Resource, the class of all resources

rdfs:Class, the class of all classes

rdfs:Literal, the class of all literals (strings)

rdf:Property, the class of all properties

rdf:Statement, the class of all reified statements

2.5.2   Core Properties for Defining Relationships

The core properties for defining relationships are

rdf:type, which relates a resource to its class (see section 2.4.1). The resource is declared to be an instance of that class.

rdfs:subClassOf, which relates a class to one of its superclasses. All instances of a class are instances of its superclass. Note that a class may be a subclass of more than one class. As an example, the class femaleProfessor may be a subclass of both female and professor.

rdfs:subPropertyOf, which relates a property to one of its superproperties.

Here is an example stating that all apartments are residential units:

   swp:apartment refs:subClassOf swp:ResidentialUnit

Note that rdfs:subClassOf and rdfs:subPropertyOf are transitive, by definition. Also, it is interesting that rdfs:Class is a subclass of rdfs:Resource (every class is a resource), and rdfs:Resource is an instance of rdfs:Class (rdfs:Resource is the class of all resources, so it is a class!). For the same reason, every class is an instance of rdfs:Class.

2.5.3 Core Properties for Restricting Properties

The core properties for restricting properties are

rdfs:domain, which specifies the domain of a property P and states that any resource that has a given property is an instance of the domain classes.

rdfs:range, which specifies the range of a property P and states that the values of a property are instances of the range classes.

Here is an example stating that whenever any resource has an address, it is (by inference) a unit and that its value is a literal:

   swp:address rdfs:domain swp:Unit.
   swp:address refs:range rdf:Literal.

2.5.4   Useful Properties for Reification

The following are some useful properties for reification:

rdf:subject, which relates a reified statement to its subject

rdf:predicate, which relates a reified statement to its predicate

rdf:object, which relates a reified statement to its object

2.5.5   Container Classes

RDF also allows for containers to be represented in a standard way. One can represent bags, sequences, or alternatives (i.e., choice).

rdf:Bag, the class of bags,

rdf:Seq, the class of sequences,

rdf:Alt, the class of alternatives,

rdfs:Container, a superclass of all container classes, including the three preceding ones.

2.5.6   Utility Properties

A resource may be defined and described in many places on the web. The following properties allow us to define links to those addresses:

rdfs:seeAlso relates a resource to another resource that explains it.

rdfs:isDefinedBy is a subproperty of rdfs:seeAlso and relates a resource to the place where its definition, typically an RDF schema, is found.

Often it is useful to provide more information intended for human readers. This can be done with the following properties:

rdfs:comment. Comments, typically longer text, can be associated with a resource.

rdfs:label. A human-friendly label (name) is associated with a resource. Among other purposes, it may serve as the name of a node in a graphic representation of the RDF document.

2.5.7   Example: Housing

We refer to the housing example, and provide a conceptual model of the domain, that is, an ontology.

```
@prefix swp: <http://www.semanticwebprimer.org/ontology/apartments.ttl#>.
@prefix rdf: <http://www.w3.org/1999/02/22-rdf-syntax-ns#>.
@prefix rdfs: <http://www.w3.org/2000/01/rdf-schema#>.


swp:Person rdf:type rdfs:Class.
swp:Person rdfs:comment "The class of people".


swp:Unit rdf:type rdfs:Class.
swp:Unit rdfs:comment "A self-contained section of accommodations
in a larger building or group of buildings.".


swp:ResidentialUnit rdf:type rdfs:Class.
swp:ResidentialUnit rdfs:subClassOf swp:Unit.
swp:ResidentialUnit
    rdfs:comment "The class of all units or places where people live.".


swp:Apartment rdf:type rdfs:Class.
swp:Apartment rdfs:subClassOf swp:ResidentialUnit.
swp:Apartment rdfs:comments "The class of apartments".
```

```
swp:House rdf:type rdfs:Class.

swp:House rdfs:subClassOf swp:ResidentialUnit.

swp:House rdfs:comment "The class of houses".


swp:residesAt rdf:type rdfs:Property.

swp:residesAt rdfs:comment "Relates persons to their residence".

swp:residesAt rdfs:domain swp:Person.

swp:residesAt rdfs:range swp:ResidentialUnit.


swp:rents rdf:type rdfs:Property.

swp:rents rdfs:comment "It inherits its domain (swp:Person)

  and range (swp:ResidentialUnit) from its superproperty (swp:residesAt)".

swp:rents rdfs:subPropertyOf swp:residesAt.


swp:address rdf:type rdfs:Property.

swp:address rdfs:comment "Is a property of units and takes literals as its value".

swp:address rdfs:domain swp:Unit.

swp:address rdfs:range rdf:Literal.
```

2.5.8   Example: Motor Vehicles

Here we present a simple ontology of motor vehicles. The class relationships are shown in figure 2.7.

```
@prefix rdf: <http://www.w3.org/1999/02/22-rdf-syntax-ns#> .

@prefix rdfs: <http://www.w3.org/2000/01/rdf-schema#> .


<#miniVan> a rdfs:Class ;

   rdfs:subClassOf <#passengerVehicle>, <#van> .
```

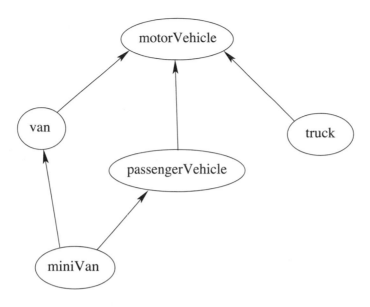

Figure 2.7: Class hierarchy for the motor vehicles example

<#motorVehicle> a rdfs:Class .

<#passengerVehicle> a rdfs:Class ;
    rdfs.subClassOf <#motorVehicle> .

<#truck> a rdfs:Class ;
    rdfs:subClassOf <#motorVehicle> .

<#van> a rdfs:Class ;
    rdfs:subClassOf <#motorVehicle> .

2.6   RDF and RDF Schema in RDF Schema

Now that we know the main components of the RDF and RDFS languages, it may be instructive to look at the definitions of RDF and RDFS. These definitions are expressed

in the language of RDF Schema. One task is to see how easily they can be read now
that the meaning of each component has been clarified.

The following definitions are just part of the full language specification. The re-
maining parts are found in the namespaces specified in rdf:RDF. We provide them in
their original XML syntax.

2.6.1   RDF

```
<?xml version="1.0" encoding="UTF-16"?>
<rdf:RDF
  xmlns:rdf="http://www.w3.org/1999/02/22-rdf-syntax-ns#"
  xmlns:rdfs="http://www.w3.org/2000/01/rdf-schema#">


<rdfs:Class rdf:ID="Statement"
  rdfs:comment="The class of triples consisting of a
             predicate, a subject and an object
             (that is, a reified statement)"/>


<rdfs:Class rdf:ID="Property"
  rdfs:comment="The class of properties"/>


<rdfs:Class rdf:ID="Bag"
  rdfs:comment="The class of unordered collections"/>


<rdfs:Class rdf:ID="Seq"
  rdfs:comment="The class of ordered collections"/>


<rdfs:Class rdf:ID="Alt"
  rdfs:comment="The class of collections of alternatives"/>
```

```
<rdf:Property rdf:ID="predicate"
rdfs:comment="Identifies the property used in a statement
            when representing the statement
            in reified form">
<rdfs:domain rdf:resource="#Statement"/>
<rdfs:range rdf:resource="#Property"/>
</rdf:Property>


<rdf:Property rdf:ID="subject"
rdfs:comment="Identifies the resource that a statement is
            describing when representing the statement
            in reified form">
<rdfs:domain rdf:resource="#Statement"/>
</rdf:Property>


<rdf:Property rdf:ID="object"
rdfs:comment="Identifies the object of a statement
            when representing the statement
            in reified form"/>


<rdf:Property rdf:ID="type"
rdfs:comment="Identifies the class of a resource.
            The resource is an instance
            of that class."/>


</rdf:RDF>
```

2.6.2 RDF Schema

```
<rdf:RDF
xmlns:rdf="http://www.w3.org/1999/02/22-rdf-syntax-ns#"
```

```
xmlns:rdfs="http://www.w3.org/2000/01/rdf-schema#">

<rdfs:Class rdf:ID="Resource"
 rdfs:comment="The most general class"/>

<rdfs:Class rdf:ID="comment"
 rdfs:comment="Use this for descriptions">
 <rdfs:domain rdf:resource="#Resource"/>
 <rdfs:range rdf:resource="#Literal"/>
</rdfs:Class>

<rdfs:Class rdf:ID="Class"
 rdfs:comment="The concept of classes.
            All classes are resources.">
 <rdfs:subClassOf rdf:resource="#Resource"/>
</rdfs:Class>

<rdf:Property rdf:ID="subClassOf">
 <rdfs:domain rdf:resource="#Class"/>
 <rdfs:range rdf:resource="#Class"/>
</rdf:Property>

<rdf:Property rdf:ID="subPropertyOf">
 <rdfs:domain rdf:resource="&rdf;Property"/>
 <rdfs:range rdf:resource="&rdf;Property"/>
</rdf:Property>


</rdf:RDF>
```

The namespaces do *not* provide the full definition of RDF and RDF Schema. Consider, for example, rdfs:subClassOf. The namespace specifies only that it applies to classes and has a class as a value. The meaning of being a subclass, namely, that all instances of one class are also instances of its superclass, is not expressed anywhere. In fact, it cannot be expressed in an RDF document. If it could, there would be no need for defining RDF Schema.

We provide a formal semantics in the next section. Of course, RDF parsers and other software tools for RDF (including query processors) must be aware of the full semantics.

2.7   An Axiomatic Semantics for RDF and RDF Schema

In this section we formalize the meaning of the modeling primitives of RDF and RDF Schema. Thus we capture the *semantics* of RDF and RDFS.

The formal language we use is *predicate logic*, universally accepted as the foundation of all (symbolic) knowledge representation. Formulas used in this formalization are referred to as *axioms*.

By describing the semantics of RDF and RDFS in a formal language like logic we make the semantics unambiguous and machine-accessible. Also, we provide a basis for reasoning support by automated reasoners manipulating logical formulas.

2.7.1   The Approach

All language primitives in RDF and RDF Schema are represented by constants: $Resource, Class, Property, subClassOf$, and so on. A few predefined predicates are used as a foundation for expressing relationships between the constants.

An auxiliary theory of lists is used. It has function symbols

nil (empty list),

$cons(x, l)$ (adds an element to the front of the list),

$first(l)$ (returns the first element),

$rest(l)$ (returns the rest of the list),

and predicate symbols

$item(x, l)$ (true iff an element occurs in the list),

$list(l)$ (true iff l is a list).

Lists are used to represent containers in RDF. They are also needed to capture the meaning of certain constructs (such as cardinality constraints) in richer ontology languages.

Most axioms provide typing information. For example,

$Type(subClassOf, Property)$

says that $subClassOf$ is a property. We use predicate logic with equality. Variable names begin with ?. All axioms are implicitly universally quantified.

Here we show the definition of most elements of RDF and RDF Schema. The axiomatic semantics of the full languages is found in an online document; see Fikes and McGuinness (2001) in suggested reading.

2.7.2   Basic Predicates

The basic predicates are

$PropVal(P, R, V)$, a predicate with three arguments, which is used to represent an RDF statement with resource R, property P, and value V

$Type(R, T)$, short for $PropVal(type, R, T)$, which specifies that the resource R has the type T

$$Type(?r, ?t) \longleftrightarrow PropVal(type, ?r, ?t)$$

2.7.3   RDF

An RDF statement (triple) (R, P, V) is represented as $PropVal(P, R, V)$.

Classes

In our language we have constants $Class, Resource, Property$, and $Literal$. All classes are instances of $Class$; that is, they have the type $Class$:

$$Type(Class, Class)$$

$$Type(Resource, Class)$$

$$Type(Property, Class)$$

$$Type(Literal, Class)$$

$Resource$ is the most general class: every object is a resource. Therefore, every class and every property is a resource:

$$Type(?p, Property) \longrightarrow Type(?p, Resource)$$

$$Type(?c, Class) \longrightarrow Type(?c, Resource)$$

Finally, the predicate in an RDF statement must be a property:

$$PropVal(?p, ?r, ?v) \longrightarrow Type(?p, Property)$$

The *type* Property

$type$ is a property:

$$Type(type, Property)$$

Note that it is equivalent to $PropVal(type, type, Property)$: the type of $type$ is $Property$. $type$ can be applied to resources and has a class as its value:

$$Type(?r, ?c) \longrightarrow (Type(?r, Resource) \land Type(?c, Class))$$

The Auxiliary *FuncProp* Property

A functional property is a property that is a function: it relates a resource to at most one value. Functional properties are not a concept of RDF but are used in the axiomatization of other primitives.

The constant $FuncProp$ represents the class of all functional properties. P is a functional property if, and only if, it is a property, and there are no x, y_1, and y_2 such that $P(x, y_1)$, $P(x, y_2)$, and $y_1 \neq y_2$.

$$Type(?p, FuncProp) \longleftrightarrow$$

$$(Type(?p, Property) \land \forall?r\forall?v1\forall?v2$$

$$(PropVal(?p, ?r, ?v1) \land PropVal(?p, ?r, ?v2) \longrightarrow ?v1 = ?v2))$$

Reified Statements

The constant $Statement$ represents the class of all reified statements. All reified statements are resources, and $Statement$ is an instance of $Class$:

$$Type(?s, Statement) \longrightarrow Type(?s, Resource)$$

$$Type(Statement, Class)$$

A reified statement can be decomposed into the three parts of an RDF triple:

$$Type(?st, Statement) \longrightarrow$$

$$\exists?p\exists?r\exists?v(PropVal(Predicate, ?st, ?p)\land$$

$$PropVal(Subject, ?st, ?r) \land PropVal(Object, ?st, ?v))$$

$Subject, Predicate$, and $Object$ are functional properties. That is, every statement has exactly one subject, one predicate, and one object:

$$Type(Subject, FuncProp)$$

$$Type(Predicate, FuncProp)$$

$$Type(Object, FuncProp)$$

Their typing information is

$$PropVal(Subject, ?st, ?r) \longrightarrow$$
$$(Type(?st, Statement) \wedge Type(?r, Resource))$$

$$PropVal(Predicate, ?st, ?p) \longrightarrow$$
$$(Type(?st, Statement) \wedge Type(?p, Property))$$

$$PropVal(Object, ?st, ?v) \longrightarrow$$
$$(Type(?st, Statement) \wedge (Type(?v, Resource) \vee Type(?v, Literal)))$$

The last axiom says, if *Object* appears as the property in an RDF statement, then it must apply to a reified statement and have as its value either a resource or a literal.

Containers

All containers are resources:

$$Type(?c, Container) \longrightarrow Type(?c, Resource)$$

Containers are lists:

$$Type(?c, Container) \longrightarrow list(?c)$$

Containers are bags or sequences or alternatives:

$$Type(?c, Container) \longleftrightarrow$$
$$(Type(?c, Bag) \vee Type(?c, Seq) \vee Type(?c, Alt))$$

Bags and sequences are disjoint:

$$\neg(Type(?x, Bag) \wedge Type(?x, Seq))$$

For every natural number $n > 0$, there is the selector $\_n$, which selects the nth element of a container. It is a functional property

$$Type(\_n, FuncProp)$$

and applies to containers only:

$$PropVal(\_n, ?c, ?o) \longrightarrow Type(?c, Container)$$

2.7.4   RDF Schema

Subclasses and Subproperties

subClassOf is a property:

$$Type(subClassOf, Property)$$

If a class C is a subclass of a class C', then all instances of C are also instances of C':

$$PropVal(subClassOf, ?c, ?c') \longleftarrow$$
$$(Type(?c, Class) \wedge Type(?c', Class) \wedge$$
$$\forall ?x(Type(?x, ?c) \longrightarrow Type(?x, ?c')))$$

Similarly for subPropertyOf: P is a subproperty of P' if $P'(x, y)$ whenever $P(x, y)$:

$$Type(subPropertyOf, Property)$$

$$PropVal(subPropertyOf, ?p, ?p') \longleftrightarrow$$
$$(Type(?p, Property) \wedge Type(?p', Property) \wedge$$
$$\forall ?r \forall ?v(PropVal(?p, ?r, ?v) \longrightarrow PropVal(?p', ?r, ?v)))$$

Constraints

Every constraint resource is a resource:

$$PropVal(subClassOf, ConstraintResource, Resource)$$

Constraint properties are all properties that are also constraint resources:

$$Type(?cp, ConstraintProperty) \longleftrightarrow$$

$$(Type(?cp, ConstraintResource) \wedge Type(?cp, Property))$$

domain and range are constraint properties:

$$Type(domain, ConstraintProperty)$$

$$Type(range, ConstraintProperty)$$

domain and range define, respectively, the domain and range of a property. Recall that the domain of a property P is the set of all objects to which P applies. If the domain of P is D, then for every $P(x, y)$, $x \in D$.

$$PropVal(domain, ?p, ?d) \longrightarrow$$

$$\forall ?x \forall ?y (PropVal(?p, ?x, ?y) \longrightarrow Type(?x, ?d))$$

The range of a property P is the set of all values P can take. If the range of P is R, then for every $P(x, y)$, $y \in R$.

$$PropVal(range, ?p, ?r) \longrightarrow$$

$$\forall ?x \forall ?y (PropVal(?p, ?x, ?y) \longrightarrow Type(?y, ?r))$$

Formulas that can be inferred from the preceding ones:

$$PropVal(domain, range, Property)$$

$$PropVal(range, range, Class)$$

$$PropVal(domain, domain, Property)$$

$$PropVal(range, domain, Class)$$

Thus we have formalized the semantics of RDF and RDFS. Software equipped with this knowledge is able to draw interesting conclusions. For example, given that the range of *rents* is *ResidentialUnit*, that *ResidentialUnit* is a subclass of *Unit*, and that *rents(JeffMeyer, BaronWayApartment)*, the agent can automatically deduce *Unit(BaronWayApartment)* using the predicate logic semantics or one of the predicate logic proof systems.

2.8   A Direct Inference System for RDF and RDFS

As stated, the axiomatic semantics detailed in section 2.7 can be used for automated reasoning with RDF and RDF Schema. However, it requires a first-order logic proof system to do so. This is a very heavy requirement and also one that is unlikely to scale when millions (or billions) of statements are involved (e.g., millions of statements of the form $Type(?r, ?c)$).

For this reason, RDF has also been given a semantics (and an inference system that is sound and complete for this semantics) directly in terms of RDF triples instead of restating RDF in terms of first-order logic, as was done in the axiomatic semantics of section 2.7.

This inference system consists of rules of the form

> IF   E contains certain triples
>
> THEN   add to E certain additional triples

(where E is an arbitrary set of RDF triples).

Without repeating the entire set of inference rules (which can be found in the official RDF documents), we give here a few basic examples:

> IF   E contains the triple $(?x, ?p, ?y)$
>
> THEN   E also contains the triple $(?p, \mathtt{rdf} : \mathtt{type}, \mathtt{rdf} : \mathtt{property})$

This states that any resource $?p$ that is used in the property position of a triple can be inferred to be a member of the class rdf:Property.

A somewhat more interesting example is the following rule:

> IF   E contains the triples $(?u, \mathtt{rdfs} : \mathtt{subClassOf}, ?v)$
>
>   and $(?v, \mathtt{rdfs} : \mathtt{subclassOf}, ?w)$
>
> THEN   E also contains the triple $(?u, \mathtt{rdfs} : \mathtt{subClassOf}, ?w)$

which encodes the transitivity of the subclass relation.

Closely related is the rule

IF   E contains the triples $(?x, \mathtt{rdf : type}, ?u)$

            and $(?u, \mathtt{rdfs : subClassOf}, ?v)$

THEN   E also contains the triple $(?x, \mathtt{rdf : type}, ?v)$

which is the essential definition of the meaning of rdfs:subClassOf.

A final example often comes as a surprise to people first looking at RDF Schema:

IF   E contains the triples $(?x, ?p, ?y)$

            and $(?p, \mathtt{rdfs : range}, ?u)$

THEN   E also contains the triple $(?y, \mathtt{rdf : type}, ?u)$

This rule states that any resource $?y$ which appears as the value of a property $?p$ can be inferred to be a member of the range of $?p$. This shows that range definitions in RDF Schema are not used to *restrict* the range of a property, but rather to *infer* the membership of the range.

The total set of these closure rules is no larger than a few dozen and can be efficiently implemented without sophisticated theorem-proving technology.

2.9 Summary

- RDF provides a foundation for representing and processing machine understandable data.

- RDF has a graph-based data model. Its key concepts are resource, property, statement, and graph. A statement is a resource-property-value triple.

- RDF has three standard syntaxes (Turtle, RDF/XML, and RDFa) to support syntactic interoperability.

- RDF has a decentralized philosophy and allows incremental building of knowledge, and its sharing and reuse.

- RDF is domain-independent. RDF Schema provides a mechanism for describing specific domains.

- RDF Schema is a primitive ontology language. It offers certain modeling primitives with fixed meaning. Key concepts of RDF Schema are class, subclass relations, property, subproperty relations, and domain and range restrictions.

Suggested Reading

The following are some official online documents:

- B. Adida and M. Birbeck. RDFa Primer: Bridging the Human and Data Webs. W3C Working Group Note. October 4, 2008.
  www.w3.org/TR/xhtml-rdfa-primer/.

- D. Beckett, ed. RDF/XML Syntax Specification (Revised). W3C Recommendation. February 10, 2004.
  www.w3.org/TR/rdf-syntax-grammar/.

- D. Beckett, T. Berners-Lee, and E. Prud'hommeaux, eds. Turtle: Terse RDF Triple Language. W3C Working Draft. August 9, 2011.
  http://www.w3.org/TR/turtle/.

- D. Brickley and R.V. Guha, eds. RDF Vocabulary Description Language 1.0: RDF Schema. W3C Recommendation. February 10, 2004.
  www.w3.org/TR/rdf-schema/.

- R. Fikes and D. McGuinness. An Axiomatic Semantics for RDF, RDF Schema and DAML+OIL. March 2001.
  www.daml.org/2001/03/axiomatic-semantics.html.

- P. Hayes, ed. RDF Semantics. W3C Recommendation. February 10, 2004.
  www.w3.org/TR/rdf-mt/.

- G. Klyne and J. Carroll, eds. Resource Description Framework (RDF): Concepts and Abstract Syntax. W3C Recommendation. February 10, 2004.
  www.w3.org/TR/rdf-concepts/.

- F. Manola and E. Miller, eds. RDF Primer. W3C Recommendation. February 10, 2004.
  www.w3.org/TR/rdf-primer/.

- E. Prud'hommeaux and A. Seaborne, eds. SPARQL Query Language for RDF. W3C Candidate Recommendation. June 14, 2007.
  www.w3.org/TR/rdf-sparql-query/.

Here are some further useful readings:

- C. Bizer and Richard Cyganiak. SPARQL The Trig Syntax.
  www4.wiwiss.fu-berlin.de/bizer/trig/.

Exercises and Projects

1. List 10 URIs that identify things in your environment.

2. Give several examples of how to extend the definition of literals in RDF. Why would this be useful?

3. Read the RDFS namespace, and try to understand the elements that were not presented in this chapter.

4. The RDFS specification allows more than one domain to be defined for a property and uses the intersection of these domains. Discuss the pros and cons of taking the union versus taking the intersection of domains.

5. In an older version of the RDFS specification, rdfs:subClassOf was not allowed to have cycles. Try to imagine situations where a cyclic class relationship would

be beneficial. (*Hint:* Think of equivalence between classes.)

6. Discuss the difference between the following statements, and draw graphs to illustrate the difference:

   X supports the proposal; Y supports the proposal; Z supports the proposal.

   The group of X, Y, and Z supports the proposal.

7. Prove the inferred formulas at the end of section 2.7 using the previous axioms.

8. Discuss why RDF and RDFS do not allow logical contradictions. Any RDF/S document is consistent; thus it has at least one model.

9. Try to map the relational database model on RDF.

10. Compare entity-relationship modeling to RDF.

11. Model part of a library in RDF Schema: books, authors, publishers, years, copies, dates, and so on. Then write some statements in RDF. Use the Turtle syntax and make sure that your RDF is syntactically valid using a validator. See http://librdf.org/parse or http://www.rdfabout.com/demo/validator/

12. Write an ontology about geography: cities, countries, capitals, borders, states, and so on.

13. Right a small web page about yourself. Identify the concepts and relations in the page and build a small ontology representing these. If possible, make use of a preexisting ontology. Mark up the page using this ontology.

In the following you are asked to think about limitations of RDFS. Specifically, what should actually be expressed, and can it be represented in RDF Schema? These limitations will be relevant in chapter 4, where we present a richer modeling language.

1. Consider the classes of males and females. Name a relationship between them that should be included in an ontology.

2. Consider the classes of persons, males, and females. Name a relationship between all three that should be included in an ontology. Which part of this relationship can be expressed in RDF Schema?

3. Suppose we declare Bob and Peter to be the father of Mary. Obviously there is a semantic error here. How should the semantic model make this error impossible?

4. What relationship exists between "is child of" and "is parent of"?

5. Consider the property *eats* with domain *animal* and range *animal or plant*. Suppose we define a new class *vegetarian*. Name a desirable restriction on *eats* for this class. Do you think that this restriction can be expressed in RDF Schema by using rdfs:range?

Chapter 3

Querying the Semantic Web

In the previous chapter, we saw how we can represent knowledge using RDF. Once information is represented in RDF, we need to be able to access relevant parts of it both for reasoning and developing applications. In this chapter, we look specifically at a query language, called SPARQL, for letting us select, extract, and otherwise easily get a hold of particular sections of knowledge expressed in RDF. SPARQL is specifically designed for RDF, and is tailored to and relies upon the various technologies underlying the web. If you are familiar with database query languages like SQL, you will notice many similarities. If you are not, this chapter does not make any assumptions and will provide everything you need to get started.

Chapter Overview

We begin the chapter by discussing the infrastructure (i.e., software) that enables SPARQL queries to be performed. We then discuss the basics of SPARQL, and progressively introduce more complex parts of it. Finally, we wrap up with a discussion of ways to collect RDF from the Semantic web.

69

3.1   SPARQL Infrastructure

To perform a SPARQL query, one needs software to execute the query. The most common software that does this is called a *triple store*. Essentially, a triple store is a database for RDF. You can download a number of triple stores online. Within the specifications for SPARQL a triple store is referred to as a Graph Store.

Before one can query a triple store, it needs to be populated with RDF. Most triple stores provide bulk upload options. There is also a mechanism called SPARQL Update, which provides a series of options for inserting and loading as well as deleting RDF into a triple store. SPARQL Update will be discussed later in the chapter.

Once data is loaded into a triple store, it can be queried by sending SPARQL queries using the SPARQL protocol. Each triple store provides what is termed an *endpoint*, where SPARQL queries can be submitted. An important point is that clients send queries to an endpoint using the HTTP protocol. Indeed, you can issue a SPARQL query to an endpoint by entering it into your browser's URL bar! However, we suggest obtaining a client designed specifically for SPARQL. Again, there are a number of them available on-line.

Because SPARQL uses standard web technologies, you will find numerous SPARQL endpoints on the web. These endpoints provide access to large amounts of data. For example, dbpedia.org/sparql provides a query endpoint to query over an RDF representation of Wikipedia. You'll find a complete list of SPARQL endpoints at CKAN.org.

Once we have this basic infrastructure, we can start writing SPARQL queries.

3.2   Basics: Matching Patterns

Recall from the previous chapter the RDF describing the Baron Way apartment and its location:

```
@prefix swp: <http://www.semanticwebprimer.org/ontology/apartments.ttl#>.
@prefix dbpedia: <http://dbpedia.org/resource/>.
@prefix dbpedia-owl: <http://dbpedia.org/ontology/>.


swp:BaronWayApartment swp:hasNumberOfBedrooms 3;
                      swp:isPartOf swp:BaronWayBuilding.
swp:BaronWayBuilding dbpedia-owl:location dbpedia:Amsterdam,
                     dbpedia:Netherlands.
```

We might like to ask a query over this data. For example: find the location of the building. How would we express this in SPARQL? We can build up this query as follows. We would want to match the following triple:

swp:BaronWayBuilding dbpedia-owl:location dbpedia:Amsterdam.

In SPARQL, we can just replace any element of the triple with a variable. Variables are denoted by a ? at their beginning. Introducing a variable for location, we would write the following:

swp:BaronWayBuilding dbpedia-owl:location ?location.

The triple store will take this *graph pattern* and try to find sets of triples that match the pattern. Thus, running this pattern over the original RDF, a triple store would return dbpedia:Amsterdam and dbpedia:Netherlands. Essentially, it finds all triples where swp:BaronWayBuilding is in the subject position and dbpedia-owl:location is in the predicate position.

To make this a complete SPARQL query, a couple of additions need to be made. First, all prefixes need to be defined. We also need to tell the triple store that we are interested in the results for a particular variable. Thus, a complete SPARQL query for the above query would be as follows:

```
PREFIX swp:     <http://www.semanticwebprimer.org/ontology/apartments.ttl#>.
PREFIX dbpedia: <http://dbpedia.org/resource/>.
PREFIX dbpedia-owl: <http://dbpedia.org/ontology/>.
SELECT ?location
WHERE {

        swp:BaronWayBuilding dbpedia-owl:location ?location.

    }
```

Like Turtle, the PREFIX keyword denotes various abbreviations for URLs. The SELECT keyword indicates which variables are of interest. The graph pattern that needs to be matched appears with brackets after the WHERE keyword. The results of the query are returned in a set of mappings called *bindings* that denote which elements correspond to a given variable. Each row in the table is a single result or binding. So for a result of this query we would get:

?location
http://dbpedia.org/resource/Amsterdam.
http://dbpedia.org/resource/Netherlands.

The whole basis of SPARQL is this simple notion of trying to find sets of triples that match a given graph pattern. SPARQL provides increasing functionality for specifying more complex patterns and providing results in different formats; but no matter how complex the pattern, the same procedure applies. Take another example: find where the BaronWayApartment is located. The SPARQL query for this is:

```
PREFIX swp:     <http://www.semanticwebprimer.org/ontology/apartments.ttl#>.
PREFIX dbpedia: <http://dbpedia.org/resource/>.
PREFIX dbpedia-owl: <http://dbpedia.org/ontology/>.
SELECT ?location
WHERE {
```

```
swp:BaronWayApartment swp:isPartOf ?building.
?building dbpedia-owl:location ?location.
}
```

We have just extended our graph pattern. There are a couple of things to note about this query: First, the variable is also in the subject position. Variables can occur in any position in the SPARQL query. Second, the query reuses the variable name ?building. In this way, the triple store knows that it should find triples where the object of the first statement is the same as the subject of the second statement. We leave it to the reader to determine the answer to the query.

We are not limited to matching a single variable. We might want to find all the information about Baron Way Apartment in the triple store. One could use this SPARQL query:

```
PREFIX swp:     <http://www.semanticwebprimer.org/ontology/apartments.ttl#>.
PREFIX dbpedia: <http://dbpedia.org/resource/>.
PREFIX dbpedia-owl: <http://dbpedia.org/ontology/>.
SELECT ?p ?o
WHERE {
        swp:BaronWayApartment ?p ?o.
}
```

Which would return the following results:

?p	?o
swp:hasNumberOfBedrooms	3
swp:isPartOf	swp:BaronWayBuilding

Again, each row in the table is a separate result that matches the graph pattern. For our rather small dataset, all possible answers can be easily returned. However, on larger

```
PREFIX swp:    <http://www.semanticwebprimer.org/ontology/apartments.ttl#>.
PREFIX dbpedia: <http://dbpedia.org/resource/>.
PREFIX dbpedia-owl: <http://dbpedia.org/ontology/>.
SELECT ?p ?o
WHERE {
      swp:BaronWayApartment ?p ?o.
}
LIMIT 10
```

Figure 3.1: A SPARQL query with LIMIT

data sets we may not know how many results there are or if our query would return a whole dataset. Indeed it is fairly easy to write queries that can return millions of triples. Therefore, it is good practice to limit the number of answers a query returns, especially when using public endpoints. This can be simply done by using the LIMIT keyword as shown in figure 3.1. In this figure, we limit the number of results to be returned to ten.

We saw before how we can match single patterns or chains of triple patterns. SPARQL provides a way of expressing concisely chains of properties. This facility is called *property paths*. Take the following example. Find all the apartments which are part of a building located in Amsterdam.

```
PREFIX swp:    <http://www.semanticwebprimer.org/ontology/apartments.ttl#>.

PREFIX dbpedia: <http://dbpedia.org/resource/>.

PREFIX dbpedia-owl: <http://dbpedia.org/ontology/>.

SELECT ?apartment

WHERE {

      ?apartment swp:isPartOf ?building.

      ?building dbpedia-owl:location dbpedia:Amsterdam.

   }
```

We can express the same thing as:

```
PREFIX ex:    <http://www.example.org/>
```

```
PREFIX dbpedia: <http://dbpedia.org/resource/>
PREFIX geo:      <http://www.geonames.org/ontology#>.
SELECT ?tournament
WHERE {

        ?apartment swp:isPartOf/dbpedia-owl:location dbpedia:Amsterdam..

     }
```

There are a number of other property paths that can be used to help express long or arbitrary paths in queries. More of these constructs will be highlighted in the chapter. However, as the reader writes more complex SPARQL these property path shortcuts may become more useful.

We can accomplish quite a bit just through matching graph patterns. However, sometimes we want to put more complex constraints on the results of our queries. In the next section, we discuss how to express those constraints using filters.

3.3   Filters

Continuing with the apartments example, let's find all the apartments that have 3 bedrooms. So far, we have seen examples where we have queried using only resources in the graph patterns but not literals. However, literals can be included in graph patterns straightforwardly. The SPARQL query is as follows:

```
PREFIX swp:     <http://www.semanticwebprimer.org/ontology/apartments.ttl#>.
PREFIX dbpedia: <http://dbpedia.org/resource/>.
PREFIX dbpedia-owl: <http://dbpedia.org/ontology/>.
SELECT ?apartment
WHERE {

        ?apartment  swp:hasNumberOfBedrooms 3.

}
```

Note that like Turtle, SPARQL allows for shortened forms of common literals. In this case, 3 is a shortcut for "3"'xsd:integer. The various syntactic shortcuts for SPARQL and Turtle are the same.

However, this query is rather contrived. In all likelihood we would want to find apartments with more or less than a certain number of bedrooms. We can ask this question in SPARQL using the FILTER keyword:

```
PREFIX swp:    <http://www.semanticwebprimer.org/ontology/apartments.ttl#>.
PREFIX dbpedia: <http://dbpedia.org/resource/>.
PREFIX dbpedia-owl: <http://dbpedia.org/ontology/>.
SELECT ?apartment
WHERE {
        ?apartment  swp:hasNumberOfBedrooms ?bedrooms.
        FILTER (?bedrooms > 2).
}
```

Resulting in:

?apartment
swp:BaronWayApartment

Less than, greater than, and equality are supported for numeric data types (i.e., integers, decimals) as well as date/time. SPARQL also allows for filtering on strings. For example, assume that our data set contains the triple:

```
swp:BaronWayApartment swp:address "4 Baron Way Circle".
```

We might like to find all the resources that contain "4 Baron Way" in their address. This can be done using the regular expressions support included within SPARQL. Regular expressions are a powerful way of expressing string searches. Describing regular expressions in detail is outside the scope of this book but the authors encourage the readers to find out more. The regular expression for finding the string "4 Baron Way" at the beginning of another string is " '4 Baron Way". This would be expressed as follows:

```
PREFIX swp:       <http://www.semanticwebprimer.org/ontology/apartments.ttl#>.
PREFIX dbpedia: <http://dbpedia.org/resource/>.
PREFIX dbpedia-owl: <http://dbpedia.org/ontology/>.
SELECT ?apartment
WHERE {
        ?apartment  swp:address ?address.
        FILTER regex(?address, "^4 Baron Way").
}
```

Here, after the FILTER keyword, a specific filter function name is introduced, regex. The parameters to that function are given in the parentheses afterwards. There are several other types of filters that SPARQL contains that may be useful in particular cases. However, the numeric and string filters are the most commonly used. One final function that is often useful is the str function. This will convert resources and literals into string representations that can then be used in regex. For example, we can search for Baron in the URL of the resource instead of using the label like this:

```
PREFIX swp:       <http://www.semanticwebprimer.org/ontology/apartments.ttl#>.
PREFIX dbpedia: <http://dbpedia.org/resource/>.
PREFIX dbpedia-owl: <http://dbpedia.org/ontology/>.
SELECT ?apartment ?address
WHERE {
        ?apartment  swp:address ?address.
        FILTER regex(str(?apartment), "Baron").
}
```

Filters provide us a mechanism for achieving flexibility. SPARQL offers more constructs to deal with the often inconsistent and varying information that is found on the Semantic Web.

3.4   Constructs for Dealing with an Open World

Unlike a traditional database, not every resource on the Semantic Web will be described using the same schema or have all of the same properties. This is called the open world assumption. For example, some apartments may be more well described than others. Furthermore, they may be described using a different vocabulary. Take the following example in RDF:

```
@prefix swp:       <http://www.semanticwebprimer.org/ontology/apartments.ttl#>.
@prefix dbpedia: <http://dbpedia.org/resource/>.
@prefix dbpedia-owl: <http://dbpedia.org/ontology/>.
@prefix xsd:       <http://www.w3.org/2001/XMLSchema#>.


swp:BaronWayApartment swp:hasNumberOfBedrooms 3.
swp:BaronWayApartment dbpedia-owl:location dbpedia:Amsterdam.
swp:BaronWayApartment refs:label "Baron Way Apartment for Rent".


swp:FloridaAveStudio swp:hasNumberOfBedrooms 1.
swp:FloridaAveStudio dbpedia-owl:locationCity dbpedia:Amsterdam.
```

In this case, the Florida Ave studio does not have a human-friendly label and its location is described using dbpedia-owl:locationCity predicate and not dbpedia-owl:location. Even with this inconsistency, we still would like to query over the data and find the apartments located in Amsterdam and return their human-friendly label if they have one. SPARQL provides two constructs for expressing such a query. Let's look at an example query:

```
PREFIX swp:    <http://www.semanticwebprimer.org/ontology/apartments.ttl#>.
PREFIX geo:    <http://www.geonames.org/ontology#>.
PREFIX dbpedia: <http://dbpedia.org/resource/>.
PREFIX dbpedia-owl: <http://dbpedia.org/ontology/>.


SELECT ?apartment ?label
WHERE {
        {?apartment  dbpedia-owl:location dbpedia:Amsterdam.}
        UNION
        {?apartment  dbpedia-owl:locationCity dbpedia:Amsterdam.}
        OPTIONAL
        {?apartment rdfs:label ?label.}
}
```

The results of this query are:

?apartment	?label
swp:BaronWayApartment	Baron Way Apartment for Rent
swp:FloridaAveStudio	

The UNION keyword tells the triple store to return results that match one or both graph patterns. The OPTIONAL keyword tells the triple store to return results for the particular graph pattern if available. That is, the graph pattern does not have to be satisfied for the query to return. Thus, in this case, without the optional, the studio apartment would not be returned in the query results.

Similarly, property paths can also be used to create a more concise SPARQL query. Using the | operator, we can express one or more possibilities. Thus, the above

SPARQL query can be rewritten as follows:

PREFIX swp: <http://www.semanticwebprimer.org/ontology/apartments.ttl#>.

PREFIX dbpedia: <http://dbpedia.org/resource/>.

PREFIX dbpedia-owl: <http://dbpedia.org/ontology/>.

SELECT ?apartment ?label

WHERE {

    {?apartment dbpedia-owl:location|dbpedia-owl:locationCity dbpedia:Amsterdam.}

    OPTIONAL

    {?apartment rdfs:label ?label.}

}

These are just some examples of how SPARQL is designed to easily query knowledge coming from different sources.

3.5   Organizing Result Sets

It is often the case that we want the results of our queries to be returned in a particular
way, either grouped, counted, or ordered. SPARQL supports a number of functions
to help us organize our results sets. We already saw how we can limit the number of
results using the the LIMIT keyword. We can also eliminate duplicate results from
the results set using the DISTINCT keyword by placing it after the select keyword
(e.g., SELECT DISTINCT ?name WHERE). This will ensure that only unique variable
bindings are returned.

SPARQL also enables the ordering of a returned result set using the ORDER BY
keyword. For example, we can ask for the apartments ordered by the number of bedrooms.

PREFIX swp: <http://www.semanticwebprimer.org/ontology/apartments.ttl#>.

PREFIX dbpedia: <http://dbpedia.org/resource/>.

PREFIX dbpedia-owl: <http://dbpedia.org/ontology/>.

SELECT ?apartment ?bedrooms

WHERE {

      ?apartment swp:hasNumberOfBedrooms ?bedrooms.

}

ORDER BY DESC(?bedrooms)

Which would return:

?apartment	?bedrooms
swp:BaronWayApartment	3
swp:FloridaAveStudio	1

The keyword DESC denotes descending order. Likewise, ASC denotes ascending order. Also, note that ordering a string or url is done alphabetically.

We can also collect results set together using *aggregate* functions. In particular, we can count the number of results (COUNT), sum over them (SUM), as well as compute the minimum, maximum, and average (MIN, MAX, AVG). Here is an example to compute the average number of bedrooms in our dataset.

PREFIX swp: <http://www.semanticwebprimer.org/ontology/apartments.ttl#>.

PREFIX dbpedia: <http://dbpedia.org/resource/>.

PREFIX dbpedia-owl: <http://dbpedia.org/ontology/>.

SELECT (AVG(?bedrooms) AS ?avgNumRooms)

WHERE {

      ?apartment swp:hasNumberOfBedrooms ?bedrooms.

}

This will return:

?avgNumRooms
2

The aggregate function is combined with the keyword AS to denote the variable in the result set. We are not limited to applying these aggregations over the entire result set. We can also aggregate for particular groups using the GROUP BY keyword.

SPARQL thus provides powerful mechanisms for organizing results in a way that best suits the application at hand.

3.6   Other Forms of SPARQL Queries

So far, we have focused on selecting certain values from a set of RDF. SPARQL also supports some other forms of queries. The two queries that are commonly used besides SELECT are ASK and CONSTRUCT.

The ASK form of query simply checks to see whether a graph pattern exists in a data set instead of returning a result. For example, the query below would return true.

```
PREFIX swp:    <http://www.semanticwebprimer.org/ontology/apartments.ttl#>.
PREFIX dbpedia: <http://dbpedia.org/resource/>.
PREFIX dbpedia-owl: <http://dbpedia.org/ontology/>.
ASK ?apartment
WHERE {
        ?apartment  swp:hasNumberOfBedrooms 3.
}
```

ASK queries are used because they are faster to compute than retrieving an entire set of results.

The CONSTRUCT form of query is used to retrieve an RDF graph from a larger set of RDF. Thus, one can query a triple store and retrieve not a list of variable bindings but an RDF graph. For example, we can create a new graph that labels big apartments as those having more than 2 bedrooms.

PREFIX ex: <http://www.example.org/>

PREFIX dbpedia: <http://dbpedia.org/resource/>

PREFIX geo: <http://www.geonames.org/ontology#>

CONSTRUCT {?apartment swp:hasNumberOfBedrooms ?bedrooms. ?apartment swp:isBigApartment true.}

WHERE{

       ?apartment   swp:hasNumberOfBedrooms ?bedrooms.

}

FILTER (?bedrooms > 2)

This would return the following graph.

@prefix swp: <http://www.semanticwebprimer.org/ontology/apartments.ttl#>.

@prefix dbpedia: <http://dbpedia.org/resource/>.

@prefix dbpedia-owl: <http://dbpedia.org/ontology/>.

@prefix xsd: <http://www.w3.org/2001/XMLSchema#>.

swp:BaronWayApartment swp:hasNumberOfBedrooms 3.

swp:BaronWayApartment swp:isBigApartment true.

CONSTRUCT queries are often used to translate between schemas by querying for particular patterns and substituting in properties from the target schema.

3.7   Querying Schemas

Importantly, because schema information is represented in RDF, SPARQL can be used to query information about the schema itself. For example, the following is part of the housing ontology from the previous chapter.

```
@prefix swp: <http://www.semanticwebprimer.org/ontology/apartments.ttl#>.

@prefix rdf: <http://www.w3.org/1999/02/22-rdf-syntax-ns#>.

@prefix rdfs: <http://www.w3.org/2000/01/rdf-schema#>.


swp:Unit rdf:type rdfs:Class.


swp:ResidentialUnit rdf:type rdfs:Class.

swp:ResidentialUnit rdfs:subClassOf swp:Unit.


swp:Apartment rdf:type rdfs:Class.

swp:Apartment rdfs:subClassOf swp:ResidentialUnit.
```

Using SPARQL, we can determine the Residential Units in our dataset by querying both the instance data and schema simultaneously:

```
PREFIX swp: <http://www.semanticwebprimer.org/ontology/apartments.ttl#>.

PREFIX rdfs:    <http://www.w3.org/2000/01/rdf-schema#> .


SELECT ?athlete

WHERE{

    ?apartment a ?unitType.

    ?unitType rdfs:subClassOf swp:ResidentialUnit.

}
```

Notice that we used the same Turtle shorthand, a, to denote rdf:type. The ability to query over the schema is an important capability of SPARQL and RDF as it allows one not only to retrieve information, but also to query the semantics of that information.

3.8   Adding Information with SPARQL Update

As mentioned in section 3.1, SPARQL also defines a protocol to update the contents of a triple store. This is the SPARQL Update protocol. Essentially, it adds a series of new keywords to SPARQL that allow for the insertion, loading, and deleting of triples. Below we show examples of each type of request.

Inserting and Loading Triples   The following inserts a statement that says Luxury Apartment is a subclass of Apartment. It appends the triple to whatever content was already in the triple store.

```
PREFIX swp: <http://www.semanticwebprimer.org/ontology/apartments.ttl#>.
PREFIX rdfs:    <http://www.w3.org/2000/01/rdf-schema#> .


INSERT DATA
{
    swp:LuxuryApartment rdfs:subClassOf swp:Apartment.
}
```

Note that the data itself is just the Turtle syntax that we are familiar with from chapter 2.

If you have a large file containing RDF available on the web, you can load it into a triple store using the following command:

```
LOAD <http://example.com/apartment.rdf>
```

Deleting Triples   There are a couple of ways to delete triples from a triple store. One is to specify exactly what triples you want to delete using the DELETE DATA keywords. Deleting the triples inserted above would look like this:

```
PREFIX swp: <http://www.semanticwebprimer.org/ontology/apartments.ttl#>.
PREFIX rdfs:    <http://www.w3.org/2000/01/rdf-schema#> .


DELETE DATA
{
    swp:LuxuryApartment rdfs:subClassOf swp:Apartment.
}
```

Note that in this form no variables are allowed and all triples must be fully specified.

For a more flexible form, one can use the DELETE WHERE construct. This removes the triples that are matched by the specified graph pattern. The following would remove all the triples containing information about apartments with more than two bedrooms.

```
PREFIX swp: <http://www.semanticwebprimer.org/ontology/apartments.ttl#>.
PREFIX rdfs:    <http://www.w3.org/2000/01/rdf-schema#> .


WHERE{
      ?apartment  swp:hasNumberOfBedrooms ?bedrooms.
      FILTER (?bedrooms > 2)
}
```

In both cases if the pattern is not matched or the triples are not in the triple store then nothing happens.

Finally, to remove all the contents of a triple store the CLEAR construct can be used as follows:

```
CLEAR ALL
```

SPARQL Update provides several more constructs for managing parts of triple stores. The update operations are particularly useful if one is progressively adding data to a triple store. In the following section, we discuss a particular case where such update operations are useful.

3.9   The Follow Your Nose Principle

SPARQL provides facilities to query and update triple stores. But how do these triple stores get populated? As mentioned earlier, many data providers make their data available via SPARQL endpoints. However, other data providers only make their data available as Linked Data. That is, RDF data made available either as files on the web or embedded in web pages. We can insert these triples into our local triples store. However, the Semantic Web allows any provider to describe their information using other resources and information on the web. In these cases, the *follow your nose principle* can be applied: Given a URL that points to some RDF, one can dereference that URL and load the corresponding data. One can continue to do so until there are enough triples to answer the given query.

Some query engines such as SQUIN implement this feature (see http://squin.sourceforge.net/). Also, the newer version of SPARQL includes commands for such federated querying. However, such federated querying is often time intensive because the data must be collected at query time.

Following your nose is one way to collect the information needed to process a query using the Semantic Web.

3.10   Summary

In this chapter, we introduced SPARQL, both its query and update portions, as well as the basic infrastructure that supports SPARQL.

- SPARQL selects information by matching graph patterns, and provides facilities for filtering based on both numeric and string comparisons.

- SPARQL queries follow a syntax similar to Turtle.

- Both data and schemas can be queried using SPARQL.

- UNION and OPTIONAL are constructs that allow SPARQL to more easily deal with open world data.

- SPARQL Update provides mechanisms for updating and deleting information from triples stores.

Suggested Reading

ARQ SPARQL Tutorial. http://jena.sourceforge.net/ARQ/Tutorial/.

S. Harris and A. Seaborne, eds. SPARQL 1.1 Query Language. W3C Working Draft (work in progress), 12 May 2011.
http://www.w3.org/TR/sparql11-query/.

A. Polleres, P. Gearon, and A. Passant, eds. SPARQL 1.1 Update. W3C Working Draft (work in progress), 12 May 2011. www.w3.org/TR/sparql11-update/.

E. Torres, L. Feigenbaum, and K. Clark, eds. SPARQL Protocol for RDF. W3C Recommendation, 15 January 2008. www.w3.org/TR/rdf-sparql-protocol/.

Exercises and Projects

1. Take one of the queries given in this chapter. Draw a diagram of the underlying data as a graph. Draw a second diagram labeling the variables from the selected query. Can you express the query as a diagram as well?

2. Think about what makes a SPARQL query difficult for a triple store to answer. Discuss what factors play into the difficulty in answering a query.

3. Compare SPARQL and SQL. What are the differences and similarities in the languages?

4. Perform several queries on http://www.dbpedia.org using one of the provided web interfaces to perform the queries: http://dbpedia.org/snorql/ or http://dbpedia.org/sparql. Discuss what is difficult about building the queries.

5. Download and install a triple store. Examples include 4store, Virtuoso, Sesame, and OWLIM. Load RDF available at the book's website (www.semanticwebprimer.ord) and see if you can answer all the queries in this chapter. If the triple store supports reasoning, do the answers to the queries change depending on the results?

6. Discuss how SPARQL uses other web standards (e.g., HTTP).

7. What is the benefit of an ontology in building SPARQL queries?

8. For a larger assignment, work in teams of 2 to 4 to develop a web application. Use an ontology from the previous chapter as its basis. For example, one could develop an apartment or book finding application. Instead of a standard database as data storage, use a triple store. We suggest using the rdfquery javascript library (http://code.google.com/p/rdfquery/) to interact with the triple store from web pages. Also, a PHP (Hypertext Preprocessor) engine such as RAP (http://www4.wiwiss.fu-berlin.de/bizer/rdfapi/) is another option. Once the application is built, write a report identifying the strengths and weaknesses of using both an ontology and a triple store for web applications.

Chapter 4

Web Ontology Language: OWL2

4.1 Introduction

The variety of things you can say in RDF and RDF Schema that we discussed in the previous chapters is deliberately very limited. RDF is (roughly) limited to binary ground predicates, and RDF Schema is (roughly) limited to a subclass hierarchy and a property hierarchy, with domain and range definitions of these properties. The languages are designed with flexibility in mind.

However, in many cases we need to express more advanced, more 'expressive,' knowledge – for example, that every person has exactly one birth date, or that no person can be both male and female at the same time.

Successive W3C working groups,[1] the Web Ontology Working Group and the OWL Working Group, identified a number of characteristic use cases for the Semantic Web that require much more language features than those that RDF and RDFS have

---

[1] See   www.w3.org/2001/sw/WebOnt/   and   http://www.w3.org/2007/OWL/wiki/OWL_ Working_ Group, respectively.

to offer. The resulting language, OWL2, for the Web Ontology Language, is closely related to a fragment of a family of logics that are specially crafted for representing terminological knowledge. These Description Logics (DL) have a long history, and their features are well understood by the community. OWL2 is the second iteration of the OWL language.

Chapter Overview

In this chapter, we first describe the motivation for OWL2 in terms of its requirements (section 4.2) and its relation with RDF and RDFS (section 4.3). We then describe the various language elements of OWL2 in detail in section 4.4, followed by a discussion of three OWL2 *profiles* (section 4.5).

4.2   Requirements for Ontology Languages

We have seen in the previous chapters that RDF and RDFS allow us to describe classes, or 'concepts,' that exist in a domain, and share these descriptions across the web. An explicit formal specification of the concepts in a domain is called an *ontology*. Languages that allow us to express ontologies are therefore called *ontology languages*. The main requirements for these languages are: a well-defined syntax, a formal semantics, sufficient expressive power, convenience of expression, and efficient reasoning support.

4.2.1   Syntax

The importance of a *well-defined syntax* is clear and known from the area of programming languages; it is a necessary condition for machine processing of information. A syntax is well-defined if you can use it to write down everything a language allows you to express in an unambiguous manner. All the languages we have presented so far have a well-defined syntax. As we will see, OWL2 builds on RDF and RDFS and uses an extension of their syntax.

A well-defined syntax is not necessarily very user-friendly. For instance, the RDF/XML syntax is notoriously hard for people to read. However, this drawback is not very significant because most ontology engineers will use specialized ontology development tools, rather than a text editor, for building ontologies.

4.2.2 Formal Semantics

A *formal semantics* describes the meaning of a language precisely. *Precisely* means that the semantics does not refer to subjective intuitions, nor is it open to different interpretations by different people (or machines). The importance of a formal semantics is well-established in the domain of mathematical logic, for instance.

The combination of formal semantics with a well-defined syntax allows us to *interpret* sentences expressed using the syntax: we now *know* what is meant by the sentence. Formal semantics also allows us to reason about the knowledge expressed in the sentences. For instance, the formal semantics of RDFS allows us to reason about *class membership*. Given:

```
:x rdf:type      :C .
:C rdfs:subClassOf :D .
```

we can infer that :x is an instance of :D. The rdfs:domain and rdfs:range properties allow similar inferences:

```
:p rdfs:range     :D .
:x :p             :y .
```

allows us to infer that :y rdf:type :D.

4.2.3 Expressivity

Unfortunately, the *expressive power* of RDF and RDFS is very limited in some areas. We often need to provide more precise definitions than what RDF and RDFS allow us to state. If we build ontologies, we may want to be able to reason about:

Class Membership We have seen that RDFS has some simple mechanisms for determining class membership of individual instances using subclass and domain and ranges. However, a more precise description of the conditions under which an instance can be considered to belong to a class would allow for more fine-grained reasoning. For instance, if we have declared that certain property-value pairs are a sufficient condition for membership in a class :A, then if an instance :x satisfies these conditions, we can conclude that :x must be an instance of :A: something is only a tennis match if it involves at least players, rackets, etc.

Classification Similarly, we would like to use the conditions on class membership to infer relations between the classes themselves. For instance, a simple definition of a tennis match can be reused to define badminton matches.

Equivalence and Equality It can be very useful to express *equivalence* between classes. For example, the class :Tortoise shares all its members with the class :Land_Turtle; they are therefore equivalent. Similarly, we would like to be able to state when two instances are the same: the :morning_star and the :evening_star are names for the same planet :venus; these instances are therefore the same. Again, being able to express this directly is nice, but it should also be possible to determine equivalence and equality by applying formal semantics to the description of our classes.

Disjointness and Difference Analogously, sometimes we know that two classes do not share any instances (they are *disjoint*) or that two instances are decidedly not the same thing. For example, :Winner and :Loser are disjoint, and :roger_federer and :rafael_nadal are different individuals.

Boolean Combinations of Classes Sometimes classes need to be combined in ways that go beyond subclass relations. For instance, we may want to define the class :Person to be the disjoint union of the classes :Female and :Male.

Local Scope of Properties rdfs:range states that the instances in the range of a property, say :plays, all belong to a certain class. Thus in RDFS we cannot declare range restrictions that differentiate between contexts. For example, we cannot say that tennis players play only tennis, while other people may play badminton.

Special Characteristics of Properties Sometimes it is useful to say that a property is *transitive*, such as :greater_than; *unique*, like :is_mother_of; or the *inverse* of another property, such as :eats and :is_eaten_by.

Cardinality Restrictions Sometimes we need to place restrictions on how many distinct values a property may or must take. For example, each person has exactly two parents, and a course is taught by at least one lecturer.

Consistency Once we can determine relations between classes, we may also want to determine conflicts between their definitions. Suppose we have declared :Fish and :Mammal to be disjoint classes. It is then an error to assert that :dolphin is an instance of both. A sufficiently expressive ontology language should allow us to detect these types of inconsistencies.

Finally, an ontology language must make it as *convenient* as possible to build sentences that make use of its expressiveness. For instance, a language is not very convenient if we would need to reiterate entire definitions every time we want to state that two classes are equivalent.

4.2.4   Reasoning Support

Formal semantics is a prerequisite for *reasoning support*. Derivations such as the preceding ones can be made mechanically instead of by hand. Automatic reasoning is important because it allows us to check the correctness of the ontology. For instance:

- check the consistency of the ontology

- check for unintended relations between classes

- check for unintended classifications of instances

Automated reasoning support allows one to check many more cases than could be checked manually. Checks like the preceding ones are extremely valuable for designing large ontologies, for cases where multiple authors are involved, and for integrating and sharing ontologies from various sources.

We can provide formal semantics and reasoning support to an ontology language by mapping it to a known logical formalism, and by using automated reasoners that already exist for those formalisms.

It is clear that we need an ontology language that is richer than RDF Schema, a language that offers these features and more. In designing such a language one should be aware of the trade-off between expressive power and efficient reasoning support. Generally speaking, the richer the logical formalism, the less efficient the reasoning support becomes, often crossing the border of decidability; that is, reasoning on such logics is not guaranteed to terminate. We therefore need a compromise, a language that can be supported by reasonably efficient reasoners, while being sufficiently expressive to represent a large variety of knowledge.

4.3   Compatibility of OWL2 with RDF/RDFS

Ideally, OWL2 is an extension of RDF Schema, in the sense that OWL2 adopts the RDFS meaning of classes and properties (rdfs:Class, rdfs:subClassOf, etc.) and adds language primitives to support the richer expressiveness required. This approach would be consistent with the layered architecture of the Semantic Web (see figure 1.4).

Unfortunately, simply extending RDF Schema would work against obtaining expressive power and efficient reasoning. RDF Schema has some very powerful modeling primitives. Constructions such as rdfs:Class (the class of all classes) and rdfs:Property (the class of all properties) are very expressive and would lead to uncontrollable computational properties if the logic underlying OWL2 included these primitives in their generality.

4.3.1   Two Semantics

The full set of requirements for an ontology language seems unobtainable: efficient reasoning support does not exist for a language as expressive as a combination of RDF Schema with a full logic. Indeed, these requirements have prompted the successive W3C working groups to split OWL2 into two different sublanguages, each with a different underlying semantics geared toward fulfilling different aspects of the full set of requirements.[2]

4.3.1.1   OWL2 Full: RDF-Based Semantics

The entire language is called OWL2 Full and uses all the OWL2 language primitives. It also allows the combination of these primitives in arbitrary ways with RDF and RDF Schema. This includes the ability to change the meaning of the predefined (RDF or OWL2) primitives by applying the language primitives to each other. For instance,

---

[2]The first version of OWL included a third sublanguage, called "OWL Lite." However, this language has been superseded by the "profiles" discussed in section 4.5.

in OWL2 Full, we could impose a cardinality constraint on the class of all classes, essentially limiting the number of classes that can be described in any ontology.

The advantage of OWL2 Full is that it is mapped to an *RDF-based semantics*. It is therefore both structurally and semantically fully upward-compatible with RDF: any legal RDF document is also a legal OWL2 Full document, and any valid RDF Schema inference is also a valid OWL2 Full conclusion. The disadvantage of OWL2 Full is that the language has become so powerful as to be undecidable, dashing any hope of complete (or efficient) reasoning support.

4.3.1.2   OWL2 DL: Direct Semantics

In order to regain computational efficiency, the second sublanguage OWL2 DL is mapped onto a description logic (DL). Description logics are a subset of predicate logic for which efficient reasoning support is possible. OWL2 DL restricts the way in which the primitives of OWL2, RDF, and RDFS may be used. Some of these restrictions are:

- OWL2 DL does not allow the application of OWL2's primitives to each other.

- Secondly, OWL2 DL can only define classes of non-literal resources. All OWL2 DL classes are instances of owl:Class rather than rdfs:Class.

- Thirdly, OWL2 DL strictly separates properties for which the range includes non-literal resources from those that relate to literal values. All OWL2 DL properties are instances of either owl:ObjectProperty or owl:DatatypeProperty but not both.

- Finally, in OWL2 DL a resource cannot be a class, property, or instance at the same time. They may share the same name (this is called "punning") but will always be treated as distinct things by the underlying logic.

The above restrictions ensure that the language maintains its direct correspondence to a well-understood description logic. Figure 4.1 shows the subclass relationships

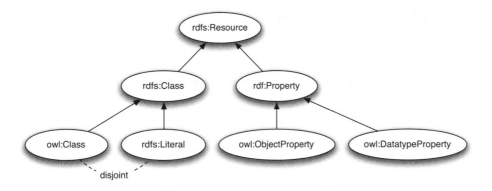

Figure 4.1: Subclass relationships between OWL2 and RDF/RDFS

between some modeling primitives of OWL2 and RDF/RDFS.

The advantage of this limited expressiveness is that it permits efficient reasoning support. OWL2 DL can make use of a wide range of existing reasoners such as Pellet, FaCT, RACER, and HermiT. The disadvantage is that we lose full compatibility with RDF. An RDF document will in general have to be extended in some ways and restricted in others before it is a legal OWL2 DL document. However, every legal OWL2 DL document is a legal RDF document.

One of the main motivations behind the layered architecture of the Semantic Web (see figure 1.4) is a hope for downward compatibility with corresponding reuse of software across the various layers. However, the advantage of full downward compatibility for OWL2 (any OWL2-aware processor will also provide correct interpretations of any RDF Schema document) is only achieved with OWL2 Full, at the cost of computational intractability.

In section 4.5 we will continue this discussion in relation to three additional *profiles* of OWL2, each of which seeks a different trade-off between expressiveness and efficient reasoning.

4.4   The OWL Language

This section introduces the language primitives of OWL2. Because of its close affinity
with formal logic, it is convenient to adopt some of the related vocabulary:

- In OWL2, the members of classes are commonly called *individuals* rather than
  instances, but we will use the two terms interchangeably.

- When we state that some resource is of a certain type, we call this an *assertion*.
  For instance:

  :roger_federer rdf:type :Person .

  is a *class assertion* relating the individual :roger_federer to its class.

- When we combine classes, properties, and instances, they form *expressions*. For
  instance:

  _:x rdf:type owl:Class ;
      owl:unionOf (:Man :Woman) .

  is a *class expression* that specifies the (anonymous) union of the classes :Man
  and :Woman.

- If we then relate this definition to one of our classes, we create an *axiom*. For
  example:

  :Person owl:equivalentClass _:x .

  _:x   rdf:type   owl:Class ;
          owl:unionOf   (:Man :Woman) .

  is an equivalent class *axiom* that states that the class :Person is equivalent to the
  union we introduced above. Class axioms are sometimes called *restrictions*, as
  they constrain the set of individuals that can be a member of a class.

It is useful to keep in mind that OWL2 is essentially a language for describing *sets* of things. These sets are called 'classes.' Any statement we make about a class in OWL2 is meant to differentiate that class from the set of *all* things.

4.4.1 Syntax

OWL2 builds on RDF and RDF Schema and thus can be expressed using all valid RDF syntaxes. However, many syntaxes exist for OWL2, each of which has its own benefits and drawbacks:

Functional-Style Syntax This syntax closely relates to the formal structure of ontologies. It is used in the language specification document, in the definitions of the semantics of OWL2 ontologies, the mappings from and into RDF syntaxes, and the different profiles of OWL2. It is much more compact and readable than many of the other syntaxes. For instance, the above class restriction can be written in this syntax as:

EquivalentClasses(:Person ObjectUnionOf(:Man :Woman))

OWL/XML This is an XML syntax for OWL2 that does not follow the RDF conventions, but closely maps onto the functional-style syntax.[3] The main benefit of this syntax is that it allows us to interact with ontologies using standard off-the-shelf XML authoring tools. For example, the OWL/XML syntax of the equivalent class axiom is:

```
<EquivalentClasses>
    <Class abbreviatedIRI=":Person"/>
    <ObjectUnionOf>
        <Class IRI="#Man"/>
```

---

[3]This OWL/XML serialization is defined in http://www.w3.org/TR/owl-xml-serialization/. It should not be confused with the older OWL/XML presentation syntax (defined in http://www.w3.org/TR/owl-xmlsyntax), which was based on the Abstract Syntax of the first version of OWL.

```
    <Class IRI="#Woman"/>
  </ObjectUnionOf>
</EquivalentClasses>
```

Manchester Syntax Originally developed by the University of Manchester, this syntax is designed to be as human-readable as possible. It is the syntax used in the user interface of most current ontology editors such as Protégé.

```
Class: Person
  EquivalentTo: Man or Woman
```

In addition to these syntaxes, all RDF syntaxes can be used for OWL. Therefore, in this chapter, we will keep using the Turtle syntax introduced in the preceding chapters.

4.4.2   Ontology Documents

When using the Turtle syntax, OWL2 ontology documents, or simply *ontologies*, are just like any other RDF document. OWL2 ontologies minimally introduce the following namespaces:

```
@prefix owl:  <http://www.w3.org/2002/07/owl#> .
@prefix rdf:  <http://www.w3.org/1999/02/22-rdf-syntax-ns#> .
@prefix rdfs: <http://www.w3.org/2000/01/rdf-schema#> .
@prefix xsd:  <http://www.w3.org/2001/XMLSchema#> .
```

An OWL2 ontology starts with a collection of assertions for housekeeping purposes. These assertions introduce a base namespace, the ontology itself, its name, possible comments, version control, and inclusion of other ontologies. For example:

```
@prefix : <http://www.semanticwebprimer.org/ontologies/apartments.ttl#> .
@prefix dbpedia-owl: <http://dbpedia.org/ontology/> .
@prefix dbpedia:     <http://dbpedia.org/resource/> .
```

```
@base       <http://www.semanticwebprimer.org/ontologies/apartments.ttl> .
```

```
<http://www.semanticwebprimer.org/ontologies/apartments.ttl>
    rdf:type       owl:Ontology ;
    rdfs:label      "Apartments Ontology"^^xsd:string ;
    rdfs:comment    "An example OWL2 ontology"^^xsd:string ;
    owl:versionIRI <http://www.semanticwebprimer.org/ontologies/apartments.ttl#1.0> ;
    owl:imports    <http://dbpedia.org/ontology/> ;
    owl:imports    <http://dbpedia.org/resource/> .
```

Imports Only one of these assertions has any consequences for the logical meaning of the ontology: owl:imports, which points to other ontologies whose axioms are to be part of the current ontology. Our apartments ontology imports all axioms defined in the DBPedia ontology, as well as *everything* in DBPedia itself. This immediately highlights one of the problems with the owl:imports: in order to be able to use *some* of the information in DBPedia, we have to import all 672 million triples described in it.[4]

While namespaces are used only for disambiguation, imported ontologies provide definitions that can be used. Typically an ontology contains an import statement for every namespace it uses, but it is possible to import additional ontologies – for example, ontologies that provide definitions without introducing any new names. The owl:imports property is *transitive*; that is, if ontology O_i imports ontology O_j, and ontology O_j imports ontology O_k, then ontology O_i also imports ontology O_k.

4.4.3 Property Types

We discussed in section 4.3.1 that OWL2 distinguishes two types of properties: *object* properties and *datatype* properties. In fact, there are a number of characteristics of properties for which additional types are provided by OWL2. In this section we briefly

---

[4]See http://dbpedia.org/About for the current status.

discuss each of these types.

Object Properties   These properties relate individuals to other individuals. Examples are :rents and :livesIn:

```
:rents rdf:type            owl:ObjectProperty ;
     rdfs:domain          :Person ;
     rdfs:range           :Apartment ;
     rdfs:subPropertyOf :livesIn .
```

Datatype Properties   These properties relate individuals to literal values of a certain data type. Examples are :name and :age:

```
:age rdf:type    owl:DatatypeProperty ;
     rdfs:range xsd:nonNegativeInteger .
```

Just as in RDF, OWL2 allows one to use XML Schema datatypes for indicating the type of a literal or specifying the range of a datatype property.[5] User-defined datatypes can be specified in an XML schema and then used in an OWL2 ontology (see section 4.4.6).

Because of the restrictions of the direct semantics, of the following property types only the *functional property* type can be assigned to datatype properties in OWL2 DL.

Annotation Properties   Annotation properties are properties that do not carry any meaning under the direct semantics of OWL2 DL. That is, they are ignored by a DL reasoner. However, they will be taken into account by RDF Schema and OWL2 Full reasoners.

Annotation properties are typically used for adding readable labels, comments, or explanations to OWL2 ontologies, classes, properties, and individuals:

---

[5]OWL2 introduces two additional datatypes owl:real and owl:rational defined as super types of xsd:decimal.

```
:label        rdf:type          owl:AnnotationProperty .

              rdfs:range        rdf:PlainLiteral .

              rdfs:subPropertyOf rdf:label


:Apartment    :label            "Apartment"@en,

                                "Appartement"@nl,

                                "Διαμέρισμα"@el .
```

There are a couple of things going on in the above example. We first define the :label property to be of type owl:AnnotationProperty with a range of rdf:PlainLiteral. This is a special RDF datatype for natural language text – that is, plain literals can have a language tag. We furthermore define the :label property to be a subproperty of rdf:label, and then give three labels to the :Apartment class in English, Dutch, and Greek.

In the general case, annotation properties will have literal values, but they may be used to relate non-literal resources as well.

Top and Bottom Properties All object properties in OWL2 are a subproperty of owl:topObjectProperty. This property is defined as the property that relates *all* individuals in the ontology. Conversely, owl:bottomObjectProperty is the property that relates *no* individuals. Similarly, owl:topDataProperty relates all individuals to any possible literal value, and owl:bottomDataProperty relates no individual to any literal value.

Transitive Properties From the discussion of rdfs:subClassOf we know that this relation is *transitive*; every class is a subclass of all superclasses of its direct superclass. Clearly there are other relations which are transitive as well, such as :isPartOf or :isCheaperThan. We can define a property as transitive as follows:

```
:isPartOf rdf:type owl:ObjectProperty ;
      rdf:type owl:TransitiveProperty .
```

When is a property composite?
<ul><li>The *top* and *bottom* properties are all composite.</li><li>Any property that is itself *transitive* or has an *inverse* property that is transitive.</li><li>Any property that has a *transitive* subproperty, or a subproperty the *inverse* of which is transitive.</li><li>Any property that is the superproperty of a *property chain*, or is an *inverse* property of a superproperty of a property chain.</li><li>Any property that is an *equivalent* property of one of the above, or is the superproperty of a property that is equivalent to one of the above.</li></ul>Composite properties are sometimes called complex roles or non-simple properties.
Restrictions
Composite properties may not occur in the following *axioms*:<ul><li>Qualified and non-qualified *cardinality* restrictions on classes;</li><li>*Self* restrictions on classes,</li><li>*Disjoint* property axioms.</li></ul>They may furthermore not be assigned the following *property types*:<ul><li>Functional or inverse functional;</li><li>Irreflexive;</li><li>Asymmetric.</li></ul>

Table 4.1: Restrictions on composite properties

Transitive properties are so-called *composite* properties: they can be said to be composed of multiple steps. For instance, given:

```
:BaronWayApartment  :isPartOf :BaronWayBuilding .
:BaronWayKitchen    :isPartOf :BaronWayApartment .
```

a reasoner will infer :

```
:BaronWayKitchen    :isPartOf :BaronWayBuilding .
```

This last :isPartOf relation is composed of the two preceding property assertions. Because of this composition, transitive properties are subject to a number of restrictions listed in table 4.1.

Symmetric and Asymmetric Properties   Some properties, such as :isAdjacentTo, are *symmetric*; that is, if a :isAdjacentTo b, the inverse holds as well. In other words, symmetric properties are equivalent to their inverse (see 4.4.4). For other properties we know that this will never be the case. For instance, the :isCheaperThan relation is *asymmetric*, since nobody can be defeated by the person they defeated.[6]

```
:isAdjacentTo  rdf:type owl:ObjectProperty ;
        rdf:type owl:SymmetricProperty .


:isCheaperThan rdf:type owl:ObjectProperty ;
        rdf:type owl:AsymmetricProperty ;
        rdf:type owl:TransitiveProperty .
```

Functional and Inverse-Functional Properties For some properties we know that every individual can always have at most one other individual related via that property. For instance, :hasNumberOfRooms is a *functional* property, and the :hasRoom property is *inverse-functional*:

```
:hasNumberOfRooms rdf:type owl:DatatypeProperty ;
        rdf:type owl:FunctionalProperty .


:hasRoom        rdf:type owl:ObjectProperty ;
        rdf:type owl:InverseFunctionalProperty .
```

Note that if two apartments a_1 and a_2 are related via :hasRoom to the same room r, this is not necessarily inconsistent: the individuals will simply be inferred to be the *same*.

Reflexive and Irreflexive Properties Reflexivity of a property means that every individual is related via that property to itself. For instance, everything :isPartOf itself. Irreflexivity, on the other hand, means that no individual is related to itself via that property. Most properties with disjoint domain and range are actually irreflexive. An example is the :rents property:

---

[6]Of course, this is only the case if every pair of persons is only allowed to compete in a single match.

```
:isPartOf      rdf:type owl:ObjectProperty ;
               rdf:type owl:ReflexiveProperty .


:rents         rdf:type owl:ObjectProperty ;
               rdf:type owl:IrreflexiveProperty .
```

4.4.4　Property Axioms

In addition to the property types discussed in the preceding section, we can specify additional characteristics of properties in terms of how they relate to classes and other properties. Some of these are familiar from RDF Schema; others are completely new.

Domain and Range　As we have seen in section 4.4.3, the way in which OWL2 treats domain and range for properties is exactly the same as in RDF Schema. If more than one rdfs:range or rdfs:domain is asserted for a property, the actual range or domain is the *intersection* of the classes specified in the property axiom.

A common misunderstanding is that domain and range work as a constraint on the types of individuals that *may* be related via a property. In fact, domains and ranges can only be used to *determine* class membership for these individuals. Given the above definition of :rents, any two individuals p and a such that p :rents a will be classified as members of :Person and :Apartment respectively.

Inverse Properties　OWL2 allows us to define the inverse of properties. A typical example is the pair :rents and :isRentedBy. For instance:

```
:isRentedBy rdf:type      owl:ObjectProperty ;
            owl:inverseOf :rents .
```

This means that a reasoner will determine that our two individuals p and m have the relation m :isRentedBy p in addition to p :rents m. Domain and range are inherited from the inverse property: :isRentedBy has :Person as range and :Apartment as domain. In OWL2 DL, only object properties can have an inverse.

Equivalent Properties   Properties can also be defined as equivalent. That is, every two individuals related via a property will always be related via its equivalent, and vice versa. Equivalence is a convenient mechanism for *mapping* elements of different ontologies to each other. For instance:

```
:isPartOf  rdf:type            owl:ObjectProperty ;
        owl:equivalentProperty dbpedia:partOf .
```

Disjoint Properties   For some properties we know that no two individuals related via one property can be related via the other: the sets of pairs of individuals for which the properties can hold are *disjoint*. Examples are the :rents and :owns properties.

```
:rents rdf:type            owl:ObjectProperty ;
       rdfs:domain          :Person ;
       rdfs:range           :Apartment ;
       owl:disjointProperty :owns .
```

Clearly, you cannot rent something you own. Note that under the direct semantics of OWL2 DL, the owl:ObjectProperty and owl:DatatypeProperty are disjoint as well.

Property Chains   A more complex feature of OWL2 is the ability to define *chains* of properties. Sometimes it is useful to specify shortcuts along the graph of properties relating various individuals. For instance, if we know that :Paul :rents the :BaronWayApartment, and that the :BaronWayApartment :isPartOf the :BaronWayBuilding, for which the dbpedia:location is dbpedia:Amsterdam, we know that :Paul must have a :livesIn relation with :Amsterdam. In OWL2 we can specify this using a property chain axiom:

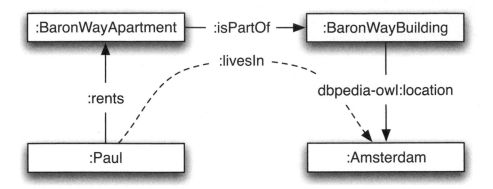

Figure 4.2: Property chains (dotted lines are inferred by the reasoner)

```
:livesIn rdf:type              owl:ObjectProperty ;
     owl:propertyChainAxiom ( :rents :isPartOf :location ) .
```

Figure 4.2 shows how the existence of the :livesIn relation can be inferred from the apartment example. Note that the property chain axiom does *not* make the named property (:livesIn) equivalent to the chain of properties; it is rather a *subproperty* of the chain. In OWL2 DL, property chains may only involve object properties, though most reasoners can handle chains that have a datatype property as last step.

Because of their expressiveness, property chains are subject to a number of restrictions. First of all, just like transitive properties, the superproperty of property chains is *composite*. This means that they cannot be used in a number of axioms (see table 4.1). Secondly, the property chain may not be recursive: the superproperty of the chain, its inverse, or one of its *sub*properties (or their inverse) may not occur in the property chain axiom. For instance, OWL2 DL does *not* allow us to extend the :livesIn property in the following way:

```
:livesIn rdf:type              owl:ObjectProperty ;
     owl:propertyChainAxiom ( :rents :isPartOf dbpedia-owl:location ) ;
     owl:propertyChainAxiom ( :livesIn dbpedia-owl:country ) .
```

even though it would allow us to infer that because :Paul lives in dbpedia:Amsterdam, he must live in dbpedia:Netherlands as well.

4.4.5 Class Axioms

Classes are defined by asserting a resource to be of type owl:Class. There are two pre-defined classes that play an important role in reasoning: owl:Thing and owl:Nothing. The former is the most *general* class; every possible OWL2 individual is a member of this class, and every instance of owl:Class is a subclass of owl:Thing. The owl:Nothing class is the *empty* class; it has no members, and every instance of owl:Class is a su-perclass of that class. Inconsistent classes cannot have any members, and are therefore equivalent to owl:Nothing. Note that restrictions on owl:Thing have very far-reaching consequences: they hold for every class and individual in the ontology.

Subclass Relations   Subclass relations are defined as in RDF Schema. For example, we can define a class :LuxuryApartment as follows:

```
:LuxuryApartment rdf:type        owl:Class ;
                 rdfs:subClassOf  :Apartment .
```

Class Equivalence   Equivalence of classes means that every member of a class must also be a member of the equivalent class, and vice versa. In other words, both classes cover exactly the same set of individuals. Class equivalence can be defined using an owl:equivalentClass property:

```
:Apartment     owl:equivalentClass dbpedia:Apartment .
```

This states that the :Apartment class in our apartment ontology is equivalent to the dbpedia:Apartment imported from DBPedia. Asserting an equivalence relation be-tween classes is equivalent to asserting subclass relations in both directions:

```
:Apartment        rdfs:subClassOf dbpedia:Apartment .
dbpedia:Apartment rdfs:subClassOf :Apartment .
```

Intermezzo: Punning   You may have noticed that the DBPedia apartment definition comes from the dbpedia namespace instead of from dbpedia-owl. It is not really a class, but an individual.

Compared to our ontology, DBPedia describes apartments at a higher level of abstraction. The classes in the DBPedia ontology are not intended to classify individual entities (such as apartments in Amsterdam), but rather individual *topics*. Treating individuals as classes is called *meta-modeling*.

Although the direct semantics of OWL2 do not allow for meta-modeling, OWL2 DL circumvents this limitation by a syntactic trick called *punning*, or 'word play.' This means that whenever the URI dbpedia:Apartment appears in a class axiom, it is treated as a class, and when it appears in an individual assertion, it is treated as individual.

Punning is allowed in the following situations: *class* names, *individual* names, and *property* names may be freely interchanged. However, *object* property names and *datatype* property names may not mix.

Enumerations   The most straightforward (though inexpressive and computationally expensive) way to define a class is by explicitly enumerating all individuals it consists of:

```
:BaronWayRooms rdf:type        owl:Class;
          owl:oneOf     ( :BaronWayKitchen
                          :BaronWayBedroom1
                          :BaronWayBedroom2
                          :BaronWayBedroom3
                          :BaronWayLivingroom
                          :BaronWayBathroom
                          ... ) .
```

This defines the class of all apartments in Amsterdam. Arguably, this type of class definition can be very cumbersome if the list of known members is very long, or even impossible if we do not currently know all individuals. For instance, we may decide to knock down the wall between :BaronWayBedroom1 and :BaronWayBedroom2, creating a new room.

Disjoint Classes Disjointness of classes means that no member of one class can also be a member of the other class. The sets of individuals described by the classes do not overlap. We can say that the :LuxuryApartment class is disjoint from :ColdWaterFlat using the owl:disjointWith property:[7]

:LuxuryApartment owl:disjointWith :ColdWaterFlat .

This means that no :LuxuryApartment can be a :ColdWaterFlat at the same time.

Complement The complement C of a class A is the class of *all* things not belonging to A. In other words, the union of A and C is equivalent to owl:Thing. Note that this means that the complement is always a superclass of the disjoint classes of A. It is important to keep in mind that complementarity is a very powerful modeling construct that should be used with care. For instance:

:FurnishedApartment rdfs:subClassOf :Apartment .
:UnFurnishedApartment rdfs:subClassOf :Apartment ;
                      owl:complementOf :FurnishedApartment .

This states that the class of furnished apartments is the complement of the class of apartments without furnishing. This is problematic if our ontology contains other classes besides apartments. For instance, if we additionally state:

---

[7]A cold water flat is an apartment which has no running hot water.

:SemiDetached owl:disjointWith :Apartment .

the :SemiDetached class will be empty. Why? If the class :Apartment covers both :FurnishedApartment and its complement, :Apartment will be equivalent to owl:Thing: there cannot be an individual not belonging to a class nor its complement. If we then additionally introduce a class that is disjoint with :Apartment, this class is effectively disjoint with owl:Thing. The :SemiDetached class cannot contain any individuals, and is thereby equivalent to owl:Nothing.

Union and Disjoint Union   We often know for some class that it is equivalent to two or more other classes: every member of the class is a member of at least one of the classes in the union. This can be specified using the owl:unionOf construct. For example:

```
:Apartment    rdf:type        owl:Class ;
        owl:unionOf     ( :ColdWaterFlat
                        :LuxuryApartment
                        :PenthouseApartment
                        :StudioApartment
                        :BasementApartment
                        :FurnishedApartment
                        :UnFurnishedApartment
                ) .
```

In many cases, the member classes of the union are mutually disjoint. Of course, we can explicitly assert owl:disjointWith relations between each class, but it is more convenient to state this directly:

```
:Apartment    rdf:type          owl:Class;
        owl:disjointUnionOf (
                        :FurnishedApartment
                        :UnFurnishedApartment ) .
```

Intersection   Similarly, we can state that a class is exactly the *intersection* of two or more other classes: every member of the class is a member of each of the classes in the intersection. For example:

```
:LuxuryApartment
        rdf:type            owl:Class ;
        owl:intersectionOf ( :GoodLocationApartment
                            :LargeApartment
                            :NiceViewApartment
                            :LuxuryBathroomApartment ) .
```

This states that the :LuxuryApartment class is populated by those individual apartments that have a good location, are of large size, have a nice view, and have a luxury bathroom.

4.4.6   Class Axioms on Properties

OWL2 allows for more fine-grained control of class definitions than we have seen in the previous sections. We can specify additional class axioms that *restrict* the set of individuals that may be considered to be a member of a class by looking at their properties. This allows us, for instance, to automatically infer class membership. Class restriction axioms are attached to an owl:Class by relating them to a special type of anonymous class (an owl:Restriction, in Turtle) that collects all individuals that satisfy the restriction.

Universal Restrictions   A universal restriction on a class C and property p states that for every member of C *all* values of p belong to a certain class. In other words, the universal restriction can be used to specify a range for a property that is local to the restricted class. This type of restriction is built using the owl:allValuesFrom construct. For example:

:LuxuryBathroomApartment

    rdf:type   owl:Class;

    rdfs:subClassOf [rdf:type   owl:Restriction;

                    owl:onProperty   :hasBathroom ;

                    owl:allValuesFrom :LuxuryBathroom

                ] .

This defines the :LuxuryBathroomApartment class as a subclass of the set of individuals that only have instances of :LuxuryBathroom as value for the :hasBathroom property. Note that an owl:allValuesFrom restriction merely states that *if* a member of the restricted class has a value for the property, then that value must be a member of the specified class. The restriction does not require the property to have any value at all: in that case, the restriction is trivially satisfied. In our apartment example, the above definition does not require that a luxury bathroom apartment have a bathroom at all!

Universal restrictions can also be used with datatype properties – for instance, to state that the value of a property must be of a certain type or fall within a certain data range (see below).

Existential Restrictions   An existential restriction on a class C and property p states that for every member of C there exists at least *some* value for p that belongs to a certain class. This type of restriction is specified using an owl:someValuesFrom keyword:

:LuxuryBathroomApartment

    rdf:type   owl:Class;

    rdfs:subClassOf [rdf:type   owl:Restriction;

                    owl:onProperty   :hasBathroom ;

                    owl:someValuesFrom :LuxuryBathroom

                ] .

Necessary and Sufficient Conditions   Instead of using the rdfs:subClassOf property to relate our class to the restriction, we could also have used an owl:equivalentClass property to state that the restricted class is exactly the class described by the restriction. The rdfs:subClassOf restriction states *necessary* conditions for class membership, while the owl:equivalentClass restriction states *necessary and sufficient* conditions.

In general, a reasoner can only directly infer class membership for individuals based on both necessary and sufficient conditions. For instance, the existential restriction above will not make a reasoner conclude that every individual that has a :hasBathroom relation with an individual of type :LuxuryBathroom must be an instance of :LuxuryBathroomApartment. The apartment is only a *subclass* of the restriction, and we do not have enough information to determine whether the individual is also a member of the class itself. If we make the class *equivalent* to the class specified by the restriction, it is clear that any individual that satisfies the restriction must also be a member of the class.

However, in both cases, if we explicitly assert an individual to be an instance of the :LuxuryBathroomApartment class, the reasoner *will* infer that there is at least some (unknown) individual of type :LuxuryBathroom as value for the :hasBathroom property.

Value Restrictions   Value restrictions come in handy when we want to define a class based on relations with known individuals, or specific values for datatype properties. For example, we can define the class of all apartments in Amsterdam:

```
:AmsterdamApartment
     rdf:type            owl:Class;
     owl:equivalentClass  [ rdf:type         owl:Restriction;
                            owl:onProperty  dbpedia-owl:location ;
                            owl:hasValue     dbpedia:Amsterdam
                          ] .
```

Cardinality Restrictions   A cardinality restriction constrains the number of values a certain property may have for a class. If we additionally specify the class these values need to belong to, the restriction is said to be *qualified*. For example:

```
:StudioApartment
          rdf:type            owl:Class;
          rdfs:subClassOf  [ rdf:type          owl:Restriction;
                             owl:onProperty    :hasRoom ;
                             owl:cardinality   "1"^^xsd:integer
                           ] .
```

This specifies that a studio apartment can have exactly one value for the :hasRoom property. We can turn this into a qualified cardinality restriction by stating that the cardinality holds for members of the :LivingRoom, :Kitchen, and :Bedroom classes only (studios do tend to have separate bathrooms):

```
:StudioApartment
          rdf:type            owl:Class;
          rdfs:subClassOf  [ rdf:type                  owl:Restriction;
                             owl:onProperty            :isPlayedBy ;
                             owl:qualifiedCardinality "1"^^xsd:integer ;
                             owl:onClass [ owl:unionOf (:LivingRoom :Kitchen :Bedroom) ]
                           ] .
```

Note that the qualified restriction still allows for the members of the restricted class to have additional values for the property, provided that these belong to the complement of the qualifier class. A qualified cardinality restriction on owl:Thing is equivalent to a restriction without qualifier. Table 4.2 summarizes the different cardinality restrictions allowed in OWL2.

Data Range Restrictions and Datatypes   Universal and existential restrictions on datatype properties allow members of a class to have *any* value from the specified

Type of restriction	Qualified	Not qualified
Exact cardinality	owl:qualifiedCardinality	owl:cardinality
Minimum cardinality	owl:qualifiedMinCardinality	owl:minCardinality
Maximum cardinality	owl:qualifiedMaxCardinality	owl:maxCardinality

Table 4.2: Cardinality restrictions in OWL2

datatype as value for the property. Sometimes we need more precise definitions to define, for instance, the class of adults who can rent apartments, or the minimum size of apartments. In OWL2, we can specify restrictions on the range of values allowed for a property:

```
:Adult    rdfs:subClassOf   dbpedia:Person ;
        rdfs:subClassOf [ rdf:type        owl:Restriction ;
                    owl:onProperty :hasAge ;
                    owl:someValuesFrom
                    [ rdf:type        rdfs:Datatype ;
                      owl:onDatatype xsd:integer ;
                      owl:withRestrictions (
                      [ xsd:minInclusive "18"^^xsd:integer ]
                      )
                    ]
        ] .
```

This defines :Adult as the subclass of persons that have a value for the :hasAge that falls within the range of integers equal to or larger than 18. You can see that the data range is defined as an anonymous class of type rdfs:Datatype. We could also have introduced a new *named* datatype that we could reuse throughout the ontology:

```
:AdultAge rdf:type            rdfs:Datatype ;
        owl:onDatatype        xsd:integer ;
        owl:withRestrictions (
            [ xsd:minInclusive "18"^^xsd:integer ]
                ) .
```

```
:Adult    rdf:type          owl:Class ;
          rdfs:subClassOf   dbpedia:Person ;
          rdfs:subClassOf [ rdf:type          owl:Restriction ;
                            owl:onProperty    :hasAge ;
                            owl:someValuesFrom :AdultAge
                          ] .
```

OWL2 allows the use of XML Schema to define datatypes. However, only datatypes defined using XML Schema *facets* can be used in restrictions. See suggested reading for more information.

Self Restrictions We all know that good apartments will sell themselves; if it is in a good location, with a nice view, and has a proper size, you do not need to spend much time redecorating it for it to sell well. In OWL2 we can express this using a *self* restriction. For instance:

```
ex:GoodApartment
          rdf:type          owl:Class ;
          rdfs:subClassOf [ rdf:type          owl:Restriction ;
                            owl:onProperty ex:sells ;
                            owl:hasSelf    "true"^^xsd:boolean ;
                          ] .
```

This states that every instance of ex:GoodApartment is related to itself with a ex:sells property. Clearly, OWL2 DL does not allow self restrictions on datatype properties.

Keys Databases typically use keys to identify records in a table. These keys are not necessarily URIs, and it can be difficult to come up with an elegant conversion scheme. OWL2 allows us to indicate that for certain classes (read: tables) the value of a specific datatype property (or combination of properties) should be regarded as a unique identifier. For example, the combination of postcode and street address number will provide a unique identifier for any dwelling in the Netherlands:

```
:postcode       rdf:type      owl:DatatypeProperty .
:addressNumber rdf:type       owl:DatatypeProperty .


:Dwelling
        rdf:type      owl:Class ;
        owl:hasKey ( :postcode :addressNumber ) .
```

Note that the key mechanism allows us to define *inverse functional datatype properties* that are local to a class. Any two individuals of type ex:Dwelling that have the same value for the :postcode and :addressNumber must be considered to be the same. Unfortunately OWL2 DL does not allow us to specify global inverse functional datatype properties because of computational consequences.

4.4.7 Individual Facts

Now that we have a general idea of how we define properties and classes in OWL2, we turn our attention to the individual entities governed by our model. In many cases we already have a lot of knowledge about these entities and only need class axioms to infer *extra* information. Statements about individuals are usually called *assertions*.

Class and Property Assertions   Class membership and property assertions in OWL2 are stated in the same way as in RDF Schema:

```
:Apartment      rdf:type    owl:Class .


:BaronWayApartment rdf:type      :Apartment ;
          :hasNumberOfRooms "4"^^xsd:integer ;
          :isRentedBy       :Paul .
```

This introduces :BaronWayApartment as an instance of the class :Apartment. It has four rooms and is rented by :Paul. Remember that under the direct semantics of OWL2 DL, the rdf:type relations may hold only between two strictly separated levels: that of classes, and that of individuals.[8]

Identity Assertions   Because OWL2 has the open world assumption, we can never assume that two individuals with different URIs must be different entities. We might be dealing with a single individual that has multiple names. Although we have seen that in some cases we can infer identity relations automatically, it is often more convenient to state them explicitly:

```
:BaronWayApartment owl:sameAs        :PaulsApartment ;
              owl:differentFrom  :FranksApartment .
```

The list of different individuals can easily grow quite long. For instance, a small city will already contain hundreds of apartments for which we would need to assert pairwise owl:differentFrom relations. Fortunately, we can state this a bit more elegantly using the owl:AllDifferent construct:

```
_:x   rdf:type    owl:AllDifferent ;
    owl:members  ( :FranksApartment :PaulsApartment ) .
```

Negative Assertions   Sometimes we know something *not* to be the case. Making this knowledge explicit can be very valuable in an open world: ruling out possibilities often allows us to infer new knowledge. For instance, the knowledge that :BaronWayApartment is not rented by :Frank may allow us to infer that it is not :FranksApartment:

```
_:x   rdf:type           owl:NegativePropertyAssertion ;
    owl:sourceIndividual   :BaronWayApartment ;
```

---

[8]See also the discussion on punning in section 4.4.5.

```
owl:assertionProperty  :isRentedBy ;
owl:targetIndividual   :Frank .
```

If the owl:assertionProperty points to datatype property, we use owl:targetValue instead of owl:targetIndividual.

Note that if we know that an individual is not a member of a certain class, we can also state this explicitly by asserting it to be a member of that class's complement:

```
:BaronWayApartment  rdf:type  [ owl:complementOf :LuxuryApartment ] .
```

4.5 OWL2 Profiles

The OWL2 specification includes a number of so-called *profiles*: some of these are well-known subsets of the OWL2 DL specification while others are more expressive but do not have the full semantics of OWL2 Full. The motivation for providing these profiles is that many existing ontologies tend to use only a particular subset of the language constructs available in DL. A significant increase of reasoner performance can be achieved through reasoning using a less expressive language. A standard library of logical profiles with a particularly likeable tradeoff between expressiveness and computational complexity can be very useful in practice.

In particular the profiles are:

- restricted by *syntax*. The semantics of a profile's syntax is provided by the OWL2 DL specification.

- defined by logics that can handle at least some interesting inference service in polynomial time with respect to either:

  - the number of facts in the ontology, or

  - the size of the ontology as a whole.

This section gives a brief overview of the profiles defined in OWL2 and their typical application areas.

OWL2 EL   The EL profile is an extension of the $\mathcal{EL}$ description logic. Its primary strength lies in the ability to reason in polynomial time on ontologies with a large number of class axioms, and it was designed to cover the expressive power of several existing large-scale ontologies in the health care and life sciences domain (e.g., SNOMED-CT, Gene Ontology, and GALEN).[9]

OWL2 EL's primary strength is in dealing with *conjunction*s and *existential* restrictions. It is lightweight and supports sound and complete reasoning in polynomial time. The most significant difference with OWL2 DL is that it drops the @powl:allValuesFrom restriction, though it does support @prdfs:range restrictions on properties, which can have a similar effect.

OWL2 QL   Reasoners developed for OWL2 DL and OWL2 EL are optimized for reasoning on class axioms, and are relatively inefficient when dealing with ontologies that have relatively uncomplicated class definitions but contain a large number of individual assertions. The QL profile of OWL2 was developed to efficiently handle *query answering* on such ontologies, and adopts technologies from relational database management. It is based on the DL-Lite description logic and extended with more expressive features such as the property inclusion axioms (@powl:subPropertyOf) and functional and inverse-functional object properties.

OWL2 RL   The OWL2 RL profile is based on so-called Description Logic Programs and enables interaction between description logics and rules: it is the largest syntactic fragment of OWL2 DL that is implementable using rules. This is a very important

---

[9]See http://www.snomed.org, http://www.geneontology.org, and http://www.openclinical.org/prj_galen.html respectively.

feature, as rules can efficiently be run in parallel, allowing for scalable reasoning implementations.

OWL2 RL differs from the QL and EL profiles in that it provides a bridge between the DL perspective and that of OWL Full: rule reasoners can easily disregard the restrictions of OWL DL (such as the separation between classes and individuals). This means that rule implementations of OWL2 RL can implement subsets of OWL Full. Many of the most scalable reasoners for Semantic Web languages implement OWL2 RL or a very similar language called pD* or OWL-Horst. The set of rules that have to be implemented is published as part of the OWL2 RL specification.

4.6   Summary

- OWL2 extends RDF and RDF Schema with a number of very expressive language features, such as cardinality constraints, class equivalence, intersection, and disjunction.

- Formal semantics and reasoning support is provided through the correspondence of OWL with logics.

- OWL2 comes in two flavors. OWL2 DL is a language that imposes some restrictions on the combination of OWL2 and RDFS language elements to retain decidability. OWL2 Full is a fully compatible extension of RDF Schema with all OWL2 language features, but it is known to be undecidable.

- Three profiles, OWL2 EL, OWL2 QL, and OWL2 RL, are syntactic subsets that have desirable computational properties. In particular, OWL2 RL is implementable using rule-based technology and has become the de facto standard for expressive reasoning on the Semantic Web.

- OWL2 has four standard syntaxes, RDF/XML, Manchester Syntax, OWL/XML, and the Functional Style syntax.

Suggested Reading

Here are the main entry points for learning more about the OWL2 language:

- Boris Motik, Bernardo Cuenca Grau, Ian Horrocks, Zhe Wu, Achille Fokoue, and Carsten Lutz, eds. OWL 2 Web Ontology Language Profiles. www.w3.org/TR/owl2-profiles/.

- Boris Motik, Peter F. Patel-Schneider, and Bernardo Cuenca Grau, eds. OWL 2 Web Ontology Language Direct Semantics. www.w3.org/TR/owl2-direct-semantics/.

- Boris Motik, Peter F. Patel-Schneider, and Bijan Parsia, eds. OWL 2 Structural Specification and Functional-Style Syntax. www.w3.org/TR/owl2-syntax/.

- Michael Schneider, ed. OWL 2 Web Ontology Language RDF-Based Semantics. www.w3.org/TR/owl2-rdf-based-semantics/.

- W3C OWL Working Group, eds. OWL 2 Web Ontology Language Document Overview. www.w3.org/TR/owl2-overview/.

Primers and tutorials about OWL2:

- Pascal Hitzler, Markus Krötzsch, Bijan Parsia, Peter F. Patel-Schneider, and Sebastian Rudolph. OWL 2 Web Ontology Language Primer. www.w3.org/TR/owl2-primer/.

- Matthew Horridge. The Manchester Pizza Tutorial. owl.cs.manchester.ac.uk/tutorials/protegeowltutorial/.

Key publications about the logics underlying OWL2:

- Franz Baader, Sebastian Brandt, and Carsten Lutz. Pushing the EL Envelope. Proceedings of IJCAI 2005: 364–369.

- I. Horrocks, O. Kutz, and U. Sattler. The Even More Irresistible SROIQ. In Proceedings of the 10th International Conference of Knowledge Representation and Reasoning (KR-2006, Lake District UK), 2006.

- Herman J. ter Horst. Combining RDF and Part of OWL with Rules: Semantics, Decidability, Complexity. International Semantic Web Conference 2005, 668–684.

A very incomplete list of software and reasoners for developing with OWL (at the time of writing):

- CEL, an OWL reasoner optimized for the OWL2 EL profile, developed at the University of Dresden. See http://lat.inf.tu-dresden.de/systems/cel/.

- HermiT, a fast OWL reasoner for complex ontologies, developed at Oxford University. See http://www.hermit-reasoner.com.

- OWLIM, a fast OWL reasoner for the OWL2 RL profile, developed by Ontotext. See http://www.ontotext.com/owlim.

- Pellet, one of the most feature-rich OWL reasoners, developed by Clark & Parsia. See http://pellet.owldl.com.

- Protégé, the de facto editing environment for OWL ontologies, developed by Stanford University. It has several reasoners built in. See http://protege.stanford.edu.

- TopBraid Composer, an RDF-based editing environment for OWL ontologies, developed by TopQuadrant. It supports SPARQL, connection to triple stores, and inferencing using the OWLIM reasoner. See http://www.topquadrant.com/products/TB_Composer.html.

- WebPIE, a massively scalable inference engine for the ter Horst fragment of OWL (roughly OWL2 RL), developed by VU University Amsterdam. See http://www.few.vu.nl/~jui200/webpie.html.

Exercises and Projects

1. Read the online specification of OWL.

2. Give three different ways of stating that two classes are disjoint.

3. Express the fact that all mathematics courses are taught by David Billington only (no other lecturer may be involved). Also express the fact that the mathematics courses are exactly the courses taught by David Billington. Is the difference clear?

4. Strictly speaking, the notion of owl:SymmetricProperty was not needed in OWL because it could have been expressed in terms of other language primitives. Explain how this can be done. (*Hint:* Consider the inverse, too.)

5. Similar question for owl:FunctionalProperty and owl:Negative PropertyAssertion. Show how they can be expressed using other OWL language constructions.

6. Determine in general which features of OWL are necessary and which are only convenient but can be simulated by other modeling primitives.

7. Explain the relationship between the concepts FunctionalProperty, InverseFunctionalProperty, and InverseOf.

8. Explain why it is necessary to declare owl:Class as a subclass of rdfs:Class.

9. In section 2.7, we presented an axiomatic semantics for RDF. A similar axiomatic semantics can be developed for OWL. Define the axiomatic semantics

of owl:intersectionOf.

10. Define the axiomatic semantics of owl:inverseOf.

11. In this exercise you are asked to develop an axiomatic semantics for cardinality restrictions.

    (a) Define noRepeatsList. L is a "no repeats list" if there is not an element that occurs in L more than once. The concept is not part of the OWL language but will be used to count the elements for cardinality restrictions.

    (b) Define owl:minCardinality and owl:maxCardinality as properties with domain owl:Restriction and range :NonNegativeInteger.

    (c) Give an axiom that captures the meaning of minCardinality:
    If $onProperty(R, P)$ and $minCardinality(R, n)$ then x is an instance of R if, and only if, there is a "no repeats list" L of length $\geq n$, such that $P(x, y)$ for all $y \in L$.

    (d) Express the meaning of owl: maxCardinality in a similar way.

12. Look at some ontologies at http://www.co-ode.org/ontologies/.

13. Write your own ontologies in OWL2.

14 OWL2 is the latest version of the OWL language. Read the pages about the previous version (see http://www.w3.org/2004/OWL/) and some of the example ontologies. Compare the old OWL language to OWL2, paying attention both to commonalities and differences.

15. Compare the online documentation on OWL2 to those for the first version of OWL.

Chapter 5

Logic and Inference: Rules

5.1 Introduction

5.1.1 Logic and Rules

From an abstract viewpoint, the subjects of chapters 2 and 4 were related to the *representation of knowledge*: knowledge about the content of web resources, and knowledge about the concepts of a domain of discourse and their relationships (ontology).

Knowledge representation had been studied long before the emergence of the World Wide Web, in the area of artificial intelligence and, before that, in philosophy. In fact, it can be traced back to ancient Greece; Aristotle is considered to be the father of logic. Logic is still the foundation of knowledge representation, particularly in the form of *predicate logic* (also known as *first-order logic*). Here we list a few reasons for the popularity and importance of logic:

- It provides a high-level language in which knowledge can be expressed in a transparent way. And it has a high expressive power.

- It has a well-understood formal semantics, which assigns an unambiguous meaning to logical statements.

- There is a precise notion of logical consequence, which determines whether a statement follows semantically from a set of other statements (premises). In fact, the primary original motivation of logic was the study of objective laws of logical consequence.

- There exist proof systems that can automatically derive statements syntactically from a set of premises.

- There exist proof systems for which semantic logical consequence coincides with syntactic derivation within the proof system. Proof systems should be sound (all derived statements follow semantically from the premises) and complete (all logical consequences of the premises can be derived in the proof system).

- Predicate logic is unique in the sense that sound and complete proof systems do exist. More expressive logics (higher-order logics) do not have such proof systems.

- Because of the existence of proof systems, it is possible to trace the proof that leads to a logical consequence. In this sense, the logic can provide explanations for answers.

The languages of RDF and OWL2 profiles (other than OWL2 Full) can be viewed as specializations of predicate logic.

One justification for the existence of such specialized languages is that they provide a syntax that fits well with the intended use (in our case, web languages based on tags). The other major justification is that they define reasonable subsets of logic. As already mentioned, there is a trade-off between the expressive power and the computational complexity of certain logics: the more expressive the language, the less efficient the corresponding proof systems. As we stated, most OWL variants correspond to a description logic, a subset of predicate logic for which efficient proof systems exist.

Another subset of predicate logic with efficient proof systems comprises the so-called *rule systems* (also known as *Horn logic* or *definite logic programs*). A rule has the form

$$A_1, \ldots A_n \rightarrow B$$

where A_i and B are atomic formulas. In fact, there are two intuitive ways of reading such a rule:

1. If $A_1, \ldots, A_n$ are known to be true, then B is also true. Rules with this interpretation are referred to as *deductive rules*.[1]

2. If the conditions $A_1, \ldots, A_n$ are true, then carry out the action B. Rules with this interpretation are referred to as *reactive rules*.

Both views have important applications. However, in this chapter we take the deductive approach. We study the language and possible queries that one can ask, as well as appropriate answers. Also, we outline the workings of a proof mechanism that can return such answers.

It is interesting to note that description logics and Horn logic are orthogonal in the sense that neither of them is a subset of the other. For example, it is impossible to define the class of happy spouses as those who are married to their best friend in description logics. But this piece of knowledge can easily be represented using rules:

$$married(X, Y), bestFriend(X, Y) \rightarrow happySpouse(X)$$

On the other hand, rules cannot (in the general case) assert (a) negation/complement of classes; (b) disjunctive/union information (for instance, that a person is either a man or a woman); or (c) existential quantification (for instance, that all persons have a father). In contrast, OWL is able to express the complement and union of classes and certain forms of existential quantification.

---

[1]There are two ways, in principle, of applying deductive rules: from the body $(A_1, \ldots, A_n)$ to the conclusion (B) (*forward chaining*), and from the conclusion (goal) to the body (*backward reasoning*).

Then we turn our attention to another kind of rules. We give a simple example. Suppose an online vendor wants to give a special discount if it is a customer's birthday. An easy way to represent this business policy with rules is as follows:

$R1$: If birthday, then special discount.

$R2$: If not birthday, then not special discount.

This solution works properly in cases where the birthday is known. But imagine a customer who refuses to provide his birthday because of privacy concerns. In such a case, the preceding rules cannot be applied because their premises are not known. To capture this situation we need to write something like

$R1$: If birthday, then special discount.

$R2'$: If birthday is not known, then not special discount.

However, the premise of rule $R2'$ is not within the expressive power of predicate logic. Thus we need a new kind of rule system. We note that the solution with rules $R1$ and $R2$ works in cases where we have complete information about the situation (for example, either birthday or not birthday). The new kind of rule system will find application in cases where the available information is incomplete.

Predicate logic and its special cases are *monotonic* in the following sense. If a conclusion can be drawn, it remains valid even if new knowledge becomes available. But if rule $R2'$ is applied to derive "not special discount," then this conclusion may become invalid if the customer's birthday becomes known at a later stage and it happens to coincide with the purchase date. This behaviour is *nonmonotonic* because the addition of new information leads to a loss of a consequence. Thus we talk of nonmonotonic rules to distinguish them from monotonic rules (which are a special case of predicate logic). In this chapter we discuss both monotonic and nonmonotonic rules.

5.1.2   Rules on the Semantic Web

Rule technology has been around for decades, has found extensive use in practice, and has reached significant maturity. And this deployment has led to a broad variety of approaches. As a result, it is far more difficult to standardize this area in the context of the (semantic) web. A W3C working group has developed the Rule Interchange Format (RIF) standard. It is important to understand how it is different from RDF and OWL: whereas the latter are languages meant for directly representing knowledge, RIF was designed primarily for the exchange of rules across different applications. For example, an online store might wish to make its pricing, refund, and privacy policies, which are expressed using rules, accessible to intelligent agents. The Semantic Web approach is to express the knowledge in a machine-accessible way using one of the web languages we have already discussed.

Due to the underlying aim of serving as an interchange format among different rule systems, RIF combines many of their features, and is quite complex. Therefore there are some doubts as to whether it will really be used widely as the primary language for expressing knowledge. Indeed, those wishing to develop rule systems for the Semantic Web have various alternatives:

- Rules over RDF can be expressed in an elegant way using SPARQL constructs; one recent proposal in this direction is SPIN.[2]

- Those wishing to use rules in the presence of rich semantic structures can use SWRL, which couples OWL DL functionalities with certain types of rules.

- Those who wish to model in terms of OWL but use rule technology for implementation purposes may use OWL2 RL.

This plurality of approaches is the reason why this chapter looks very different from the previous ones, which were based on one, or a family of, very stable and widely

---

[2]However, SPARQL is not a rule language, as basically it carries out one application of a rule. A rule system has to be developed on top of, say, SPIN.

adopted standard(s). RIF is a step in this direction, but not yet at the same level of community agreement and adoption. Therefore, the chapter presents ideas at a generic level, and presents a number of concrete approaches.

Chapter Overview

Readers who are not comfortable with the notation and basic notions of predicate logic are advised to read some introductory chapters of logic books, like those listed at the end of this chapter. Alternatively, they may skip parts of sections 5.3 and 5.4.

- Section 5.2 provides an example using monotonic rules (that is, of the subset of predicate logic called Horn logic).

- Sections 5.3 and 5.4 describe the syntax and semantics of Horn logic.

- Section 5.5 discusses the relationship between OWL2 RL and rules.

- 5.6 presents the family of RIF dialects, with a focus on the logic-based languages.

- Section 5.7 describes SWRL as a way of combining rules with description logics.

- Section 5.8 briefly describes how rules can be modeled using SPARQL constructs.

- Section 5.9 describes the syntax of nonmonotonic rules, and section 5.10 presents an example of nonmonotonic rules.

- Finally, section 5.11 briefly describes RuleML, an ongoing activity for rule markup on the web with an open and experimental agenda that may feed into new standards in the future.

5.2 Example of Monotonic Rules: Family Relationships

Imagine a database of facts about some family relationships. Suppose that the database contains facts about the following *base predicates*:

$$mother(X, Y) \qquad X \text{ is the mother of } Y$$

$$father(X, Y) \qquad X \text{ is the father of } Y$$

$$male(X) \qquad X \text{ is male}$$

$$female(X) \qquad X \text{ is female}$$

Then we can infer further relationships using appropriate rules. First, we can define a predicate *parent*: a parent is either a father or a mother.

$$mother(X, Y) \rightarrow parent(X, Y)$$

$$father(X, Y) \rightarrow parent(X, Y)$$

Then we can define a brother to be a male person sharing a parent:

$$male(X), parent(P, X), parent(P, Y), notSame(X, Y) \rightarrow$$
$$brother(X, Y)$$

The predicate *notSame* denotes inequality; we assume that such facts are kept in a database. Of course, every practical logical system offers convenient ways of expressing equality and inequality, but we chose the abstract solution to keep the discussion general.

Similarly, *sister* is defined as follows:

$$female(X), parent(P, X), parent(P, Y), notSame(X, Y) \rightarrow$$
$$sister(X, Y)$$

An uncle is a brother of a parent:

$$brother(X, P), parent(P, Y) \to uncle(X, Y)$$

A grandmother is the mother of a parent:

$$mother(X, P), parent(P, Y) \to grandmother(X, Y)$$

An ancestor is either a parent or an ancestor of a parent:

$$parent(X, Y) \to ancestor(X, Y)$$

$$ancestor(X, P), parent(P, Y) \to ancestor(X, Y)$$

5.3   Monotonic Rules: Syntax

Let us consider a simple rule stating that all loyal customers with ages over 60 are entitled to a special discount:

$$loyalCustomer(X), age(X) > 60 \to discount(X)$$

We distinguish some ingredients of rules:

- *variables*, which are placeholders for values: X

- *constants*, which denote fixed values: 60

- *predicates*, which relate objects: $loyalCustomer$, $>$

- *function symbols*, which denote a value, when applied to certain arguments: age

In case no function symbols are used, we discuss function-free (Horn) logic.

5.3.1 Rules

A rule has the form

$$B_1, \ldots, B_n \to A$$

where $A, B_1, \ldots, B_n$ are atomic formulas. A is the *head* of the rule, and $B_1, \ldots, B_n$ are the *premises* of the rule. The set $\{B_1, \ldots, B_n\}$ is referred to as the *body* of the rule.

The commas in the rule body are read conjunctively: if B_1 and B_2 and ... and B_n are true, then A is also true (or equivalently, to prove A it is sufficient to prove all of $B_1, \ldots, B_n$).

Note that variables may occur in $A, B_1, \ldots, B_n$. For example,

$$loyalCustomer(X), age(X) > 60 \to discount(X)$$

This rule is applied for *any* customer: if a customer happens to be loyal and over 60, then she gets the discount. In other words, the variable X is implicitly universally quantified (using $\forall X$). In general, all variables occurring in a rule are implicitly universally quantified.

In summary, a rule r

$$B_1, \ldots, B_n \to A$$

is interpreted as the following formula, denoted by $pl(r)$:

$$\forall X_1 \ldots \forall X_k((B_1 \wedge \ldots \wedge B_n) \to A)$$

or equivalently,

$$\forall X_1 \ldots \forall X_k(A \vee \neg B_1 \vee \ldots \vee \neg B_n)$$

where $X_1, \ldots, X_k$ are all variables occurring in $A, B_1, \ldots, B_n$.

5.3.2   Facts

A fact is an atomic formula, such as $loyalCustomer(a345678)$, which says that the customer with ID a345678 is loyal. The variables of a fact are implicitly universally quantified.

5.3.3   Logic Programs

A logic program P is a finite set of facts and rules. Its predicate logic translation $pl(P)$ is the set of all predicate logic interpretations of rules and facts in P.

5.3.4   Goals

A goal denotes a query G asked to a logic program. It has the form

$$B_1, \ldots, B_n \rightarrow$$

If $n = 0$ we have the *empty goal* $\square$.

Our next task is to interpret goals in predicate logic. Using the ideas we have developed so far (interpretations of commas as conjunction, implicit universal quantification), we get the following interpretation:

$$\forall X_1 \ldots \forall X_k (\neg B_1 \vee \ldots \vee \neg B_n)$$

This formula is the same as $pl(r)$, with the only difference that the rule head A is omitted.[3]

An equivalent representation in predicate logic is

$$\neg \exists X_1 \ldots \exists X_k (B_1 \wedge \ldots \wedge B_n)$$

where $X_1, \ldots, X_k$ are all variables occurring in $B_1, \ldots, B_n$. Let us briefly explain this formula. Suppose we know

---

[3]Note that the formula is equivalent to $\forall X_1 \ldots \forall X_k (false \vee \neg B_1 \vee \ldots \vee \neg B_n)$, so a missing rule head can be thought of as a contradiction $false$.

$$p(a)$$

and we have the goal

$$p(X) \rightarrow$$

Actually, we want to know whether there is a value for which p is true. We expect a positive answer because of the fact $p(a)$. Thus $p(X)$ is existentially quantified. But then why do we negate the formula? The explanation is that we use a proof technique from mathematics called *proof by contradiction*. This technique proves that a statement A follows from a statement B by assuming that A is false and deriving a contradiction when combined with B. Then A *must* follow from B.

In logic programming we prove that a goal can be answered positively by negating the goal and proving that we get a contradiction using the logic program. For example, given the logic program

$$p(a)$$

and the goal

$$\neg \exists X p(X)$$

we get a logical contradiction: the second formula says that no element has the property p, but the first formula says that the value of a does have the property p. Thus $\exists X p(X)$ follows from $p(a)$.

5.4 Monotonic Rules: Semantics

5.4.1 Predicate Logic Semantics

One way of answering a query is to use the predicate logic interpretation of rules, facts, and queries, and to make use of the well-known semantics of predicate logic. To be more precise, given a logic program P and a query

$$B_1, \ldots, B_n \rightarrow$$

with the variables $X_1, \ldots, X_k$, we answer positively if, and only if,

$$pl(P) \models \exists X_1 \ldots \exists X_k (B_1 \wedge \ldots \wedge B_n) \qquad (1)$$

or equivalently, if

$$pl(P) \cup \{\neg \exists X_1 \ldots \exists X_k (B_1 \wedge \ldots \wedge B_n)\} \text{ is unsatisfiable} \qquad (2)$$

In other words, we give a positive answer if the predicate logic representation of the program P, together with the predicate logic interpretation of the query, is unsatisfiable (a contradiction).

The formal definition of the semantic concepts of predicate logic is found in the literature. Here we just give an informal presentation. The components of the logical language (signature) may have any meaning we like. A predicate logic model, $\mathcal{A}$, assigns a certain meaning. In particular, it consists of

- a *domain dom*$(\mathcal{A})$, a nonempty set of objects about which the formulas make statements,

- an element from the domain for each constant,

- a concrete function on $dom(\mathcal{A})$ for every function symbol,

- a concrete relation on $dom(\mathcal{A})$ for every predicate.

When the symbol $=$ is used to denote equality (i.e., its interpretation is fixed), we talk of *Horn logic with equality*. The meanings of the logical connectives $\neg, \vee, \wedge, \rightarrow, \forall, \exists$ are defined according to their intuitive meaning: not, or, and, implies, for all, there is. This way we define when a formula is true in a model $\mathcal{A}$, denoted as $\mathcal{A} \models \varphi$.

A formula φ *follows* from a set M of formulas if φ is true in all models $\mathcal{A}$ in which M is true (that is, all formulas in M are true in $\mathcal{A}$).

Now we are able to explain (1) and (2). Regardless of how we interpret the constants, predicates, and function symbols occurring in P and the query, once the predicate logic interpretation of P is true, $\exists X_1 \ldots \exists X_k (B_1 \wedge \ldots \wedge B_n)$ must be true, too. That is, there are values for the variables $X_1, \ldots, X_k$ such that all atomic formulas B_i become true.

For example, suppose P is the program

$p(a)$

$p(X) \rightarrow q(X)$

Consider the query

$q(X) \rightarrow$

Clearly, $q(a)$ follows from $pl(P)$. Therefore, $\exists X q(X)$ follows from $pl(P)$, thus $pl(P) \cup \{\neg \exists X q(X)\}$ is unsatisfiable, and we give a positive answer. But if we consider the query

$q(b) \rightarrow$

then we must give a negative answer because $q(b)$ does not follow from $pl(P)$.

5.4.2 Least Herbrand Model Semantics

The other kind of semantics for logic programs, least Herbrand model semantics, requires more technical treatment, and is described in standard logic textbooks (see suggested reading).

5.4.3 Ground and Parameterized Witnesses

So far we have focused on yes/no answers to queries. However, such answers are not necessarily optimal. Suppose that we have the fact

$$p(a)$$

and the query

$$p(X) \rightarrow$$

The answer yes is correct but not satisfactory. It resembles the joke where you are asked, "Do you know what time it is?" and you look at your watch and answer "yes." In our example, the appropriate answer is a substitution

$$\{X/a\}$$

which gives an instantiation for X, making the answer positive. The constant a is called a *ground witness*. Given the facts

$$p(a)$$

$$p(b)$$

there are two ground witnesses to the same query: a and b. Or equivalently, we should return the substitutions:

$$\{X/a\}$$

$$\{X/b\}$$

While valuable, ground witnesses are not always the optimal answer. Consider the logic program

$$add(X, 0, X)$$

$$add(X, Y, Z) \rightarrow add(X, s(Y), s(Z))$$

This program computes addition, if we read s as the "successor function," which returns as value the value of its argument plus 1. The third argument of add computes the sum of its first two arguments. Consider the query

$$add(X, s^8(0), Z) \rightarrow$$

Possible ground witnesses are determined by the substitutions

$$\{X/0, Z/s^8(0)\}$$

$$\{X/s(0), Z/s^9(0)\}$$

$$\{X/s(s(0)), Z/s^{10}(0)\}$$

$$\ldots$$

However, the *parameterized witness* $Z = s^8(X)$ is the most general way to witness the existential query

$$\exists X \exists Z \; add(X, s^8(0), Z)$$

since it represents the fact that $add(X, s^8(0), Z)$ is true whenever the value of Z equals the value of X plus 8.

The computation of most general witnesses is the primary aim of a proof system, called SLD resolution, the presentation of which is beyond the scope of this book.

5.5 OWL2 RL: Description Logic Meets Rules

As stated at the beginning of this chapter, Horn logic and description logics are orthogonal. In attempting to achieve their integration into one framework, the simplest approach is to consider the intersection of both logics, that is, the part of one language that can be translated in a semantics-preserving way to the other language, and vice versa. In essence, OWL2 RL seeks to capture this fragment of OWL. The advantages of this approach include:

- From the modeler's perspective, there is freedom to use either OWL or rules (and associated tools and methodologies) for modeling purposes, depending on the modeler's experience and preferences.

- From the implementation perspective, either description logic reasoners or deductive rule systems can be used. Thus it is possible to model using one framework, such as OWL, and to use a reasoning engine from the other framework, such as rules. This feature provides extra flexibility and ensures interoperability with a variety of tools.

In the remainder of this section we show how many constructs of RDF Schema and OWL2 RL can be expressed in Horn logic, and also discuss some constructs that in general cannot be expressed. This discussion focuses on the basic constructs highlighting the connections and differences between rules and description logics. For more information on OWL2 RL constructs and their relation to logic, please refer to section 5.6.4 and the suggested reading at the end of this chapter.

We begin with RDF and RDF Schema. A triple of the form (a, P, b) in RDF can be expressed as a fact

$$P(a, b)$$

Similarly, an instance declaration of the form $type(a, C)$, stating that a is an instance of class C, can be expressed as

$$C(a)$$

The fact that C is a subclass of D is easily expressed as

$$C(X) \rightarrow D(X)$$

and similarly for subproperty. Finally, domain and range restrictions can also be expressed in Horn logic. For example, the following rule states that C is the domain of property P:

$$P(X, Y) \rightarrow C(X)$$

Now we turn to OWL. $equivalentClass(C, D)$ can be expressed by the pair of rules

$$C(X) \rightarrow D(X)$$

$$D(X) \rightarrow C(X)$$

and similarly for *equivalentProperty*. Transitivity of a property P is easily expressed as

$$P(X,Y), P(Y,Z) \rightarrow P(X,Z)$$

Now we turn to Boolean operators. We can state that the intersection of classes C_1 and C_2 is a subclass of D as follows:

$$C_1(X), C_2(X) \rightarrow D(X)$$

In the other direction, we can state that C is a subclass of the intersection of D_1 and D_2 as follows:

$$C(X) \rightarrow D_1(X)$$

$$C(X) \rightarrow D_2(X)$$

For union, we can express that the union of C_1 and C_2 is a subclass of D using the following pair of rules:

$$C_1(X) \rightarrow D(X)$$

$$C_2(X) \rightarrow D(X)$$

However, the opposite direction is outside the expressive power of Horn logic. To express the fact that C is a subclass of the union of D_1 and D_2 would require a disjunction in the head of the corresponding rule, which is not available in Horn logic. Note that there are cases where the translation is possible. For example, when D_1 is a subclass of D_2, then the rule $C(X) \rightarrow D_2(X)$ is sufficient to express that C is a subclass of the union of D_1 and D_2. The point is that there is not a translation that works in all cases.

Finally, we briefly discuss some forms of restriction in OWL. The OWL statement

```
:C  rdfs:subClassOf  [ rdf:type  owl:Restriction ;
                      owl:onProperty  :P ;
                      owl:allValuesFrom  :D  ] .
```

can be expressed in Horn logic as follows:

$$C(X), P(X, Y) \rightarrow D(Y)$$

However, the opposite direction cannot be expressed in general. And the OWL statement

```
[ rdf:type           owl:Restriction ;
  owl:onProperty      :P ;
  ow:lsomeValuesFrom  :D  ] rdfs:subClassOf :C .
```

can be expressed in Horn logic as follows:

$$P(X, Y), D(Y) \rightarrow C(X)$$

The opposite direction cannot be expressed in general.

Also, cardinality constraints and complement of classes cannot be expressed in Horn logic in the general case.

5.6   Rule Interchange Format: RIF

5.6.1   Overview

Rule technology has existed for decades now, and exhibits a broad variety (e.g., action rules, first order rules, logic programming). As a consequence, the aim of the W3C Rule Interchange Format Working Group was not to develop a new rule language that would fit all purposes, but rather to focus on the interchange among the various (existing or future) rule systems on the web. The approach taken was to develop a family of languages, called *dialects*; RIF defined two kinds of dialects:

1. *Logic-based dialects.* These are meant to include rule languages that are based on some form of logic; for example, first-order logic and various logic programming approaches with different interpretations of negation (answer-set programming, well-founded semantics, etc.). The concrete dialects developed so far under this branch are:

  - *RIF Core*, essentially corresponding to function-free Horn logic; and

  - *RIF Basic Logic Dialect (BLD)*, essentially corresponding to Horn logic with equality.

2. *Rules with actions.* These are meant to include production systems and reactive rules. The concrete dialect developed so far in this branch is:

  - *Production Rule Dialect (RIF-PRD).*

The RIF family was designed to be both *uniform* and *extensible*. Uniformity is achieved by expecting the syntax and semantics of all RIF dialects to share basic principles. Extensibility refers to the possibility of future dialects being developed and added to the RIF family. For the logic-based side, the RIF Working Group proceeded to support uniformity and extensibility by developing the *Framework for Logic Dialects (RIF-FLD)* which allows one to specify various rule languages by instantiating the various parameters of the approach. This framework is a major achievement, but goes beyond the scope of this book. In the following we will present the basic ideas of RIF-BLD.

Before doing so, it should be stated that a lot, if not most, of the work of the RIF Working Group was dedicated to semantic aspects. Of course, rule interchange takes place at the syntactic level (e.g., using XML) using mappings between the various syntactic features of a logic system and RIF. But the main objective is to interchange rules in a *semantics preserving way*.

5.6.2 RIF-BLD

The RIF Basic Logic Dialect basically corresponds to Horn logic with equality plus

- data types and built ins, and

- frames.

RIF-BLD, like all other RIF variants, is expected to support a uniform set of commonly used datatypes, predicates, and functions. This set includes data types (such as *integer, boolean, string, date*), "built-in" predicates (such as *numeric-greater-than, starts-with, date-less-than*), and functions (such as *numeric-subtract, replace, hours-from-time*) ranging over these data types.

As an example, suppose we wish to express a rule stating that an actor is a movie star if he has starred in more than three successful movies, produced in a span of at least five years. And a film is considered successful if it has received critical acclaim (say, a rating higher than 8 out of 10) or was financially successful (produced more than $100 million in ticket sales). These rules should be evaluated against the DBpedia data set.

These rules can be expressed in RIF-BLD as follows:

```
Document(
    Prefix(func <http://www.w3.org/2007/rif-builtin-function#>
    Prefix(pred <http://www.w3.org/2007/rif-builtin-predicate#>
    Prefix(rdfs <http://www.w3.org/2000/01/rdf-schema#>
    Prefix(imdbrel <http://example.com/imdbrelation#>
    Prefix(dbpedia <http://dbpedia.org/ontology/>
    Prefix(ibdbrel <http://example.com/ibdbrelation#>
Group(
    Forall ?Actor ?Film ?Year (
        If And(  dbpedia:starring(?Film ?Actor)
                 dbpedia:dateOfFilm(?Film ?Year)
```

```
                Then dbpedia:starredInYear(?Film ?Actor ?Year)
    )

    Forall ?Actor (
        If ( Exists ?Film1 ?Film2 ?Film3 ?Year1 ?Year2 ?Year3
                And (    dbpedia:starredInYear(?Film1 ?Actor ?Year1)
                         dbpedia:starredInYear(?Film2 ?Actor ?Year2)
                         dbpedia:starredInYear(?Film3 ?Actor ?Year3)
                         External ( pred:numeric-greater-than(
                               External(func:numeric-subtract ?Year1 ?Year3) 5)))
                    dbpedia:successful(?Film1)
                    dbpedia:successful(?Film2)
                    dbpedia:successful(?Film3)
                    External (pred:literal-not-identical(?Film1 ?Film2))
                    External (pred:literal-not-identical(?Film1 ?Film3))
                    External (pred:literal-not-identical(?Film2 ?Film3))
                           )
                Then dbpedia:movieStar(?Actor)
    )

    Forall ?Film (
            If Or (
                    External(pred:numeric-greater-than(
                        dbpedia:criticalRating(?Film 8))
                    External(pred:numeric-greater-than(
                        dbpedia:boxOfficeGross(?Film) 100000000)))
            Then dbpedia:successful(?Film)
    )

)
```

This example demonstrates the use of data types and built ins. Note the use of *External* in applying built-in predicates. Also the use of *Group* to put together a number of rules.

The syntax of RIF is rather straightforward, though quite verbose (of course, there is also an XML-based syntax to support interchange between rule systems). Variable names begin with a question mark. And the symbols =, #, and ## are used to express equality, class membership, and subclass relationship, respectively.

The use of *frames* has a long tradition in object-oriented languages and knowledge representation, and has also been prominent in the area of rule languages (e.g., F-Logic). The basic idea is to represent objects as frames and their properties as *slots*. For example, we might have a class professor with slots such as name, office, phone, department, etc. Such information is expressed in RIF-BLD using the notation

```
oid[slot1 -> value1 ... slotn -> valuen]
```

5.6.3   Compatibility with RDF and OWL

A major feature of RIF is that it is compatible with the RDF and OWL standards. That is, one can reason with a combination of RIF, RDF, and OWL documents. Thus RIF facilitates the interchange of not just rules, but also RDF graphs and/or OWL axioms.

The basic idea of combining RIF with RDF is to represent RDF triples using RIF frame formulas; a triple *s p o* is represented as s[p -> o]. The semantic definitions are such that the triple is satisfied iff the corresponding RIF frame formula is, too. For example, if the RDF triple

```
ex:GoneWithTheWind ex:FilmYear ex:1939
```

is true, then so is the RIF fact

```
ex:GoneWithTheWind[ex:FilmYear -> ex:1939]
```

Given the RIF rule (which states that the Hollywood Production Code was in place between 1930 and 1968)

```
Group(
    Forall ?Film (
        If And(   ?Film[ex:Year -> ?Year]
                  External(pred:dateGreaterThan(?Year 1930))
                  External(pred:dateGreaterThan(1968 ?Year)))
        Then ?Film[ex:HollywoodProductionCode -> ex:True]
    )
)
```

one can conclude

```
ex:GoneWithTheWind[ex:HollywoodProductionCode -> ex:True]
```

as well as the corresponding RDF triple.

Similar techniques are used to achieve compatibility between OWL and RIF. The main features are:

- The semantics of OWL and RIF are compatible;

- One can infer conclusions from certain combinations of OWL axioms and RIF knowledge; and

- OWL2 RL can be implemented in RIF (see next section).

5.6.4   OWL2 RL in RIF

OWL2 RL is partially described by a set of first-order rules that can form the basis for an implementation using rule technology. To enable interoperability between rule systems and OWL2 RL ontologies, this axiomatization can be described using RIF (BLD, actually even in the simpler Core) rules.

The OWL2 RL rules can be categorized in four (non-disjoint) categories: triple pattern rules, inconsistency rules, list rules, and datatype rules.

Triple Pattern Rules   These rules derive certain RDF triples from a conjunction of RDF triple patterns. Translation of these rules to RIF (using Frame formulas) is straightforward using rules of the form:[4]

```
Group(
    Forall ?V1 ... ?Vn(
        s[p->o] :- And(s1[p1->o1]... sn[pn->on]))
)
```

Inconsistency Rules   Such rules indicate inconsistencies in the original RDF graph (of course w.r.t. the existing OWL knowledge). These rules can be easily represented in RIF as rules with conclusion *rif:error*, a predicate symbol within the RIF namespace that can be used to express inconsistency. For example, an inconsistency occurs when two predicates have been declared to be disjoint, but connect the same entities. This can be expressed in RIF as follows:

```
Group(
    Forall ?P1 ?P2 ?X ?Y(
        rif:error :- And(
            ?P1[owl:propertyDisjointWith ?P2] ?X[?P1->?Y] ?X[?P2->?Y]))
)
```

List Rules   A number of OWL2 RL rules involve processing OWL expressions that include RDF lists (for example *owl:AllDifferent*). Two approaches are possible to express these rules in RIF. One may use recursive rules to traverse RDF graphs at run time, yielding a uniform representation. Or one may take a preprocessing approach

---

[4]For improved readability, these rules are given in Prolog (backward) notation, instead of the If-Then (forward) notation used so far.

where rules are directly instantiated for the lists that actually occur in the input RDF graph, which may perform better in practice. Readers are referred to the translation document (see suggested reading) for details.

Datatype Rules   These rules provide type checking and value equality/inequality checking for typed literals in the supported datatypes. For example, such rules may derive *owl:sameAs* triples for literals with the same value in the datatype (e.g., 1 and 1.0), or an inconsistency if a literal is specified to be an instance of a data type but its value is outside the value space of that data type. The translation to RIF rules is rather straightforward.

5.7   Semantic Web Rules Language (SWRL)

SWRL is a proposed Semantic Web language combining OWL DL with function-free Horn logic and is written in Unary/Binary Datalog RuleML (see section 5.11). Thus it allows Horn-like rules to be combined with OWL DL ontologies.

A rule in SWRL has the form

$$B_1, \ldots, B_n \rightarrow A_1, \ldots, A_m$$

where the commas denote conjunction on both sides of the arrow and $A_1, \ldots, A_m, B_1, \ldots, B_n$ can be of the form $C(x)$, $P(x, y)$, $sameAs(x, y)$, or $differentFrom(x, y)$, where C is an OWL description, P is an OWL property, and x, y are Datalog variables, OWL individuals, or OWL data values.

If the head of a rule has more than one atom (if it is a conjunction of atoms without shared variables), the rule can be transformed to an equivalent set of rules with one atom in the head in a straightforward way.

The main complexity of the SWRL language stems from the fact that arbitrary OWL expressions, such as restrictions, can appear in the head or body of a rule. This feature adds significant expressive power to OWL, but at the high price of undecidability; that is, there can be no inference engine that draws exactly the same conclusions as the SWRL semantics.

Compared to OWL2 RL, SWRL lies at the other end of the integration of description logics and function-free rules. Where OWL2 RL uses a very conservative approach, seeking to combine the advantages of both languages in their common sublanguage, SWRL takes a more maximalist approach and unites their respective expressivities. From a practical perspective, the challenge is to identify sublanguages of SWRL that find the right balance between expressive power and computational tractability. A candidate for such a sublanguage is the extension of OWL DL with *DL-safe rules*, in which every variable must appear in a non-description logic atom in the rule body. See the articles on integrating rules with description logics in suggested reading.

As a remark, an outcome similar to SWRL can be achieved by combining RIF-BLD with OWL2 RL (see suggested reading).

5.8   Rules in SPARQL: SPIN

Rules can be expressed in SPARQL using its CONSTRUCT feature. For example, the rule

$$grandparent(X, Z) \leftarrow parent(Y, Z), parent(X, Y)$$

can be expressed as:

```
CONSTRUCT {
    ?X grandParent ?Z.
}   WHERE {
    ?Y parent ?Z.
    ?X parent ?Y.
}
```

The recent proposal SPIN takes this as a starting point to propose a modeling language over SPARQL. Its main ideas and features include:

- It uses ideas of object-oriented modeling in associating rules to classes; thus rules may represent behavior of that class, and may not exist on their own (though global rules can also be defined).

- It expresses rules by SPARQL CONSTRUCT, DELETE, and INSERT, and constraints using the SPARQL ASK construct.

- It provides abstraction mechanisms for rules using Templates, which in essence encapsulate parameterized SPARQL queries; and user-defined SPIN functions as a mechanism to build higher-level rules (complex SPAROL queries) on top of simpler building blocks.

As a proof of concept, the OWL2 RL rules have been expressed in SPIN. For example, the rule

$$C_2(X) \leftarrow C_1(X), equivalentClass(C_1, C_2)$$

can be represented in SPARQL as:

```
CONSTRUCT {
    ?X a ?C2.
}
WHERE {
    ?X a ?C1.
    ?C1 equivalentClass ?C2.
}
```

and then instantiated as a *spin:rule* for the class *owl:Thing*; this will allow the rule to be applied to all possible instances.

It should be noted that SPARQL, and thus SPIN, is a rule *language*, not an implemented rule *system*; for example, CONSTRUCT only expresses one inference step (from one RDF graph to another). A rule system on top of SPARQL (e.g., a SPIN inference engine) would need, among other things, to run CONSTRUCT iteratively and to control recursion in case of recursive rules.

5.9   Nonmonotonic Rules: Motivation and Syntax

5.9.1   Informal Discussion

Now we turn our attention to nonmonotonic rule systems. So far, once the premises of a rule were proved, the rule could be applied, and its head could be derived as a conclusion. In nonmonotonic rule systems, a rule may not be applied even if all premises are known because we have to consider contrary reasoning chains. In general, the rules we consider from now on are called *defeasible* because they can be defeated by other rules. To allow conflicts between rules, *negated atomic formulas* may occur in the head and the body of rules. For example, we may write

$$p(X) \rightarrow q(X)$$

$$r(X) \rightarrow \neg q(X)$$

To distinguish between defeasible rules and standard, monotonic rules, we use a different arrow:

$$p(X) \Rightarrow q(X)$$

$$r(X) \Rightarrow \neg q(X)$$

In this example, given also the facts

$p(a)$

$r(a)$

we conclude neither $q(a)$ nor $\neg q(a)$. It is a typical example of two rules blocking each other. This conflict may be resolved using *priorities among rules*. Suppose we knew somehow that the first rule is stronger than the second; then we could indeed derive $q(a)$.

Priorities arise naturally in practice and may be based on various principles:

- The source of one rule may be more reliable than the source of the second rule, or it may have higher authority. For example, federal law preempts state law. And in business administration, higher management has more authority than middle management.

- One rule may be preferred over another because it is more recent.

- One rule may be preferred over another because it is more specific. A typical example is a general rule with some exceptions; in such cases, the exceptions are stronger than the general rule.

Specificity may often be computed based on the given rules, but the other two principles cannot be determined from the logical formalization. Therefore we abstract from the specific prioritization principle, and assume the existence of an *external priority relation* on the set of rules. To express the relation syntactically, we extend the rule syntax to include a unique label. For example,

$r_1 : p(X) \Rightarrow q(X)$

$r_2 : r(X) \Rightarrow \neg q(X)$

Then we can write

$r_1 > r_2$

to specify that r_1 is stronger than r_2.

We do not impose many conditions on $>$. It is not even required that the rules form a complete ordering. We require only the priority relation to be acyclic. That is, it is impossible to have cycles of the form

$$r_1 > r_2 > \ldots > r_n > r_1$$

Note that priorities are meant to resolve conflicts among *competing rules*. In simple cases two rules are competing only if the head of one rule is the negation of the head of the other. But in applications it is often the case that once a predicate p is derived, some other predicates are excluded from holding. For example, an investment consultant may base his recommendations on three levels of risk that investors are willing to take: low, moderate, and high. Only one risk level per investor is allowed to hold at any given time. Technically, these situations are modeled by maintaining a conflict set $C(L)$ for each literal L. $C(L)$ always contains the negation of L but may contain more literals.

5.9.2   Definition of the Syntax

A *defeasible rule* has the form

$$r : L_1, \ldots, L_n \Rightarrow L$$

where r is the *label*, $\{L_1, \ldots, L_n\}$ the *body* (or *premises*), and L the *head* of the rule. $L, L_1, \ldots, L_n$ are positive or negative literals (a literal is an atomic formula $p(t_1, \ldots, t_m)$ or its negation $\neg p(t_1, \ldots, t_m)$). No function symbols may occur in the rule.[5] Sometimes we denote the head of a rule as $head(r)$, and its body as $body(r)$. Slightly abusing notation, sometimes we use the label r to refer to the whole rule.

A *defeasible logic program* is a triple $(F, R, >)$ consisting of a set F of facts, a finite set R of defeasible rules, and an acyclic binary relation $>$ on R (precisely, a set of pairs $r > r'$ where r and r' are labels of rules in R).

---

[5]This restriction is imposed for technical reasons, the discussion of which is beyond the scope of this chapter.

5.10 Example of Nonmonotonic Rules: Brokered Trade

This example shows how rules can be used in an electronic commerce application (which ideally will run on the Semantic Web). Brokered trades take place via an independent third party, the broker. The broker matches the buyer's requirements and the sellers' capabilities and proposes a transaction in which both parties can be satisfied by the trade.

As a concrete application we will discuss apartment renting,[6] a common activity that is often tedious and time-consuming. Appropriate web services can reduce the effort considerably. We begin by presenting the potential renter's requirements.

> Carlos is looking for an apartment of at least 45 sq m with at least two bedrooms. If it is on the third floor or higher, the house must have an elevator. Also, pet animals must be allowed.

> Carlos is willing to pay $300 for a centrally located 45 sq m apartment, and $250 for a similar apartment in the suburbs. In addition, he is willing to pay an extra $5 per square meter for a larger apartment, and $2 per square meter for a garden.

> He is unable to pay more than $400 in total. If given the choice, he would go for the cheapest option. His second priority is the presence of a garden; his lowest priority is additional space.

5.10.1 Formalization of Carlos's Requirements

We use the following predicates to describe properties of apartments:

$apartment(x)$ stating that x is an apartment

$size(x, y)$ y is the size of apartment x (in sq m)

---

[6]In this case the landlord takes the role of the abstract seller.

$$bedrooms(x, y) \qquad\qquad x \text{ has } y \text{ bedrooms}$$

$$price(x, y) \qquad\qquad y \text{ is the price for } x$$

$$floor(x, y) \qquad\qquad x \text{ is on the } y\text{th floor}$$

$$garden(x, y) \qquad\qquad x \text{ has a garden of size } y$$

$$elevator(x) \qquad\qquad \text{there is an elevator in the house of } x$$

$$pets(x) \qquad\qquad \text{pets are allowed in } x$$

$$central(x) \qquad\qquad x \text{ is centrally located}$$

We also make use of the following predicates:

$$acceptable(x) \qquad\qquad \text{flat } x \text{ satisfies Carlos's requirements}$$

$$offer(x, y) \qquad\qquad \text{Carlos is willing to pay \$ } y \text{ for flat } x$$

Now we present Carlos's firm requirements. Any apartment is a priori acceptable.

$$r_1 : apartment(X) \Rightarrow acceptable(X)$$

However, Y is unacceptable if one of Carlos's requirements is not met.

$$r_2 : bedrooms(X, Y), Y < 2 \Rightarrow \neg acceptable(X)$$

$$r_3 : size(X, Y), Y < 45 \Rightarrow \neg acceptable(X)$$

$$r_4 : \neg pets(X) \Rightarrow \neg acceptable(X)$$

$$r_5 : floor(X, Y), Y > 2, \neg lift(X) \Rightarrow \neg acceptable(X)$$

$$r_6 : price(X, Y), Y > 400 \Rightarrow \neg acceptable(X)$$

Rules r_2-r_6 are exceptions to rule r_1, so we add

$$r_2 > r_1, \; r_3 > r_1, \; r_4 > r_1, \; r_5 > r_1, \; r_6 > r_1$$

Next we calculate the price Carlos is willing to pay for an apartment.

$r_7 : size(X, Y), Y \geq 45, garden(X, Z), central(X) \Rightarrow$

$\quad offer(X, 300 + 2Z + 5(Y - 45))$

$r_8 : size(X, Y), Y \geq 45, garden(X, Z), \neg central(X) \Rightarrow$

$\quad offer(X, 250 + 2Z + 5(Y - 45))$

An apartment is only acceptable if the amount Carlos is willing to pay is not less than the price specified by the landlord (we assume no bargaining can take place).

$r_9 : offer(X, Y), price(X, Z), Y < Z \Rightarrow \neg acceptable(X)$

$r_9 > r_1$

5.10.2 Representation of Available Apartments

Each available apartment is given a unique name, and its properties are represented as facts. For example, apartment a_1 might be described as follows:

$bedrooms(a_1, 1)$

$size(a_1, 50)$

$central(a_1)$

$floor(a_1, 1)$

$\neg elevator(a_1)$

$pets(a_1)$

$garden(a_1, 0)$

$price(a_1, 300)$

The descriptions of the available apartments are summarized in table 5.1. In practice, the apartments on offer could be stored in a relational database or, in a Semantic Web setting, in an RDF storage system.

Flat	Bedrooms	Size	Central	Floor	Elevator	Pets	Garden	Price
a_1	1	50	yes	1	no	yes	0	300
a_2	2	45	yes	0	no	yes	0	335
a_3	2	65	no	2	no	yes	0	350
a_4	2	55	no	1	yes	no	15	330
a_5	3	55	yes	0	no	yes	15	350
a_6	2	60	yes	3	no	no	0	370
a_7	3	65	yes	1	no	yes	12	375

Table 5.1: Available apartments

If we match Carlos's requirements and the available apartments, we see that

- flat a_1 is not acceptable because it has one bedroom only (rule r_2);

- flats a_4 and a_6 are unacceptable because pets are not allowed (rule r_4);

- for a_2, Carlos is willing to pay \$300, but the price is higher (rules r_7 and r_9);

- flats a_3, a_5, and a_7 are acceptable (rule r_1).

5.10.3   Selecting an Apartment

So far, we have identified the apartments acceptable to Carlos. This selection is valuable in itself because it reduces the focus to relevant flats, which may then be physically inspected. But it is also possible to reduce the number further, even down to a single apartment, by taking further preferences into account. Carlos's preferences are based on price, garden size, and size, in that order. We represent them as follows:

$r_{10}: \ acceptable(X) \Rightarrow cheapest(X)$

$r_{11}: \ acceptable(X), price(X, Z), acceptable(Y), price(Y, W),$
$\qquad W < Z \Rightarrow \neg cheapest(X)$

$r_{12}: \ cheapest(X) \Rightarrow largestGarden(X)$

r_{13} : $cheapest(X), gardenSize(X, Z), cheapest(Y),$

$\qquad gardenSize(Y, W), W > Z \Rightarrow \neg largestGarden(X)$

r_{14} : $largestGarden(X) \Rightarrow rent(X)$

r_{15} : $largestGarden(X), size(X, Z), largestGarden(Y),$

$\qquad size(Y, W), W > Z \Rightarrow \neg rent(X)$

$r_{11} > r_{10}, \; r_{13} > r_{12}, \; r_{15} > r_{14}$

Rule r_{10} says that every acceptable apartment is cheapest by default. However, if there is an acceptable apartment cheaper than X, rule r_{11} (which is stronger than r_{10}) fires and concludes that X is not cheapest.

Similarly, rules r_{12} and r_{13} select the apartments with the largest garden among the cheapest apartments. And of these, rules r_{14} and r_{15} select the proposed apartments to be rented, based on apartment size.

In our example, apartments a_3 and a_5 are cheapest. Of these a_5 has the largest garden. Note that in this case the apartment size criterion does not play a role: r_{14} fires only for a_5, and rule r_{15} is not applicable. Thus a selection has been made, and Carlos will soon move in.

5.11   Rule Markup Language (RuleML)

RuleML is a long-running effort to develop markup of rules on the web. It is actually not one language but a family of rule markup languages, corresponding to different kinds of rule languages: derivation rules, integrity constraints, reaction rules, and so on. The kernel of the RuleML family is Datalog, which is function-free Horn logic.

RuleML is quite experimental in studying various features of rule languages that are far from being standardized (e.g. nonmonotonic rules). The idea is that these efforts may feed into future standards, in the same way that RuleML results were an important building block in the development of RIF.

Rule Ingredient	RuleML
fact	Asserted Atom
rule	Asserted Implies
head	then
body	if
atom	Atom
conjunction	And
predicate	Rel
constant	Ind
variable	Var

Figure 5.1: RuleML vocabulary

The RuleML family provides descriptions of rule markup languages in XML, in the form of RELAX NG or XML schemas (or document type definitions for earlier versions). The representation of rule ingredients is straightforward. Figure 5.1 describes the key vocabulary of Datalog RuleML.

The expression of rules using the RuleML vocabulary is straightforward. For example, the rule *"The discount for a customer buying a product is 7.5 percent if the customer is premium and the product is luxury"* is represented in RuleML 1.0 as follows.

```
<Implies>
    <then>
        <Atom>
            <Rel>discount</Rel>
            <Var>customer</Var>
            <Var>product</Var>
            <Ind>7.5 percent</Ind>
        </Atom>
    </then>
    <if>
        <And>
```

```
<Atom>

    <Rel>premium</Rel>

    <Var>customer</Var>

</Atom>

<Atom>

    <Rel>luxury</Rel>

    <Var>product</Var>

</Atom>

        </And>

    </if>

</Implies>
```

The language SWRL, introduced in section 5.7, is an extension of RuleML, and its use is straightforward. As an example, we show the representation of the rule

$$brother(X, Y), childOf(Z, Y) \rightarrow uncle(X, Z)$$

in the XML syntax of SWRL using RuleML 1.0.

```
<ruleml:Implies>

    <ruleml:then>

        <swrlx:individualPropertyAtom swrlx:property="uncle">

            <ruleml:Var>X</ruleml:Var>

            <ruleml:Var>Z</ruleml:Var>

        </swrlx:individualPropertyAtom>

    </ruleml:then>

    <ruleml:if>

        <ruleml:And>

            <swrlx:individualPropertyAtom swrlx:property="brother">

                <ruleml:Var>X</ruleml:Var>

                <ruleml:Var>Y</ruleml:Var>

            </swrlx:individualPropertyAtom>
```

```
<swrlx:individualPropertyAtom swrlx:property="childOf">
    <ruleml:Var>Z</ruleml:Var>
    <ruleml:Var>Y</ruleml:Var>
</swrlx:individualPropertyAtom>
        </ruleml:And>
    </ruleml:if>
</ruleml:Implies>
```

5.12   Summary

- Rules on the (semantic) web form a very rich and heterogeneous landscape.

- Horn logic is a subset of predicate logic that allows efficient reasoning. It forms a subset orthogonal to description logics. Horn logic is the basis of monotonic rules.

- RIF is a new standard for rules on the web. Its logical dialect BLD is based on Horn logic.

- OWL2 RL, which is essentially the intersection of description logics and Horn logic, can be embedded in RIF.

- SWRL is a much richer rule language, combining description logic features with restricted types of rules.

- Nonmonotonic rules are useful in situations where the available information is incomplete. They are rules that may be overridden by contrary evidence (other rules).

- Priorities are used to resolve some conflicts between nonmonotonic rules.

- The representation of rules in XML-like languages, such as those provided by RIF and RuleML, is straightforward.

Suggested Reading

Horn logic is a standard topic in logic. More information can be found in relevant textbooks, such as the following:

- E. Burke and E. Foxley. *Logic and Its Applications*. Upper Saddle River, N.J.: Prentice Hall, 1996.

- M. A. Covington, D. Nute, and A. Vellino. *Prolog Programming in Depth*, 2nd ed. Upper Saddle River, N.J.: Prentice Hall, 1997.

- A. Nerode and R. A. Shore. *Logic for Applications*. New York: Springer, 1997.

- U. Nilsson and J. Maluszynski. *Logic, Programming and Prolog*, 2nd ed. New York: Wiley, 1995.

- N. Nissanke. *Introductory Logic and Sets for Computer Scientists*. Boston: Addison-Wesley, 1998.

Nonmonotonic rules are a quite new topic. Information can be found in the second textbook above, and in the following articles:

- G. Antoniou, D. Billington, G. Governatori, and M. J. Maher. Representation Results for Defeasible Logic. *ACM Transactions on Computational Logic* 2 (April 2001): 255–287.

- N. Bassiliades, G. Antoniou, and I. Vlahavas. A Defeasible Logic Reasoner for the Semantic Web. *International Journal on Semantic Web and Information Systems* 2,1 (2006): 1–41.

- T. Eiter, T. Lukasiewicz, R. Schindlauer, and H. Tompits. Combining Answer Set Programming with Description Logics for the Semantic Web. In *Proceedings of the 9th International Conference on Principles of Knowledge Representation and Reasoning (KR'04)*, AAAI Press 2004, 141–151.

- D. Nute. Defeasible Logic. In *Handbook of Logic in Artificial Intelligence and Logic Programming Vol. 3*, ed. D. M. Gabbay, C. J. Hogger, and J. A. Robinson. New York: Oxford University Press, 1994.

Information about RIF and its compatibility with RDF and OWL is found at

- http://www.w3.org/2005/rules/wiki/Primer.

- http://www.w3.org/TR/rif-overview/.

- http://www.w3.org/TR/rif-bld/.

- http://www.w3.org/TR/rif-rdf-owl/.

An introduction to the formal foundation of RIF-BLD is found in

- M. Kifer. Knowledge Representation and Reasoning on the Semantic Web: RIF. In *Handbook of Semantic Web Technologies*, eds. J. Domingue, D. Fensel, and J. Hendler. Springer 2011.

Information about OWL2 RL and its embedding in RIF is found at

- http://www.w3.org/TR/owl2-profiles/.

- http://www.w3.org/TR/rif-owl-rl/.

Information on SPIN and its encoding of parts of OWL2 RL is found at

- http://www.w3.org/Submission/spin-overview/.

- http://topbraid.org/spin/owlrl-all.html.

Information about SWRL is found at

- www.w3.org/Submission/SWRL/.

Other important works on integrating rules with description logics are

- I. Horrocks, P. Patel-Schneider, S. Bechhofer, and D. Tsarkov. OWL Rules: A Proposal and Prototype Implementation. *Journal of Web Semantics* 3,1 (2005): 23–40.

  www.websemanticsjournal.org/ps/pub/2005-2.

- B. Motik, U. Sattler, and R. Studer. Query Answering for OWL-DL with Rules. *Journal of Web Semantics* 3,1 (2005): 41–60.

  www.websemanticsjournal.org/ps/pub/2005-3.

- R. Rosati. On the Decidability and Complexity of Integrating Ontologies and Rules. *Journal of Web Semantics* 3,1 (2005): 61–73.

  www.websemanticsjournal.org/ps/pub/2005-4.

General information about markup languages for rules and their use in the Semantic Web can be found at the RuleML website:

- www.ruleml.org/.

Exercises and Projects

The following projects use rule technology. It is assumed that readers have some knowledge and experience with basic Semantic Web technologies. If not, it may be best to work on more basic projects first (see chapter 7).

Semantic Brokering

1. This basic project can be done by two people in two or three weeks. The aim is to implement an application similar to the apartment renting example in section 5.10. The following tasks should be carried out:

(a) Select a topic in which a brokering activity is to be carried out. Here brokering refers to the matching of offerings and requirements.

(b) Build an RDFS ontology for the domain.

(c) Populate the ontology with offerings, expressed in RDF.

(d) Express the selection criteria using nonmonotonic rules.

(e) Run your rules with the RDF/RDFS information using an engine such as DR-DEVICE[7] or DR-Prolog.[8] To do so, you will need to express the rules in the format prescribed by these systems.

2. This advanced project can be carried out by two or three people over the course of a term. The aim is to implement a brokering scenario in a multi-agent environment. Apart from carrying out the steps described in project 5.4, project participants need, among other things, to:

(a) Develop a basic understanding of brokering in multi-agent environments by studying some relevant literature:

> K. Sycara, S. Widoff, M. Klusch, and J. Lu. Larks: Dynamic Matchmaking among Heterogeneous Software Agents in Cyberspace. *Autonomous Agents and Multi-Agent Systems* 5, 2 (2002): 173–203.
>
> G. Antoniou, T. Skylogiannis, A. Bikakis, and N. Bassiliades. A Deductive Semantic Brokering System. In *Proceedings of the 9th International Conference on Knowledge-Based Intelligent Information and Engineering Systems.* LNCS 3682, Springer 2005, 746–752.

(b) Choose and familiarize yourselves with a multi-agent system. We have had good experience with JADE.[9]

(c) Decide on the precise messages to be exchanged between agents.

---

[7]lpis.csd.auth.gr/systems/dr-device.html.
[8]www.csd.uoc.gr/~bikakis/DR-Prolog/.
[9]jade.tilab.com/.

(d) Find out how to remotely call the inference engine to be used.

Proof Layer

The aim of these projects is to realize a proof layer, the vision of which was briefly outlined in chapter 1. Note that there is not one proof layer, but rather a proof layer for each selected Semantic Web reasoning system (logic). Still, some considerations are common to all such systems. Two possible logical systems for which one could implement a proof layer are

- a simple monotonic rules language, such as Datalog (Horn logic without function symbols), for which the reasoning tool Mandarax[10] could be used;

- a nonmonotonic rules language, as discussed in this chapter, for which DR-DEVICE[11] or DR-Prolog[12] could be used.

3. This basic project can be done by two or three people in about two months. The aim is to develop an interactive system that provides explanation to the user. Important aspects to be addressed include the following:

(a) Decide how to extract relevant information from the overall proof trace. You could consult the automated reasoning and logic programming literature for ideas.

(b) Define levels of granularity for representing proofs. Should whole proofs be shown, or only metasteps? These could then be refined if the user questions a certain step.

(c) Ultimately, the "leaves" of a proof will be RDF facts, rules, or inference conditions used.

---

[10] mandarax.sourceforge.net/.
[11] lpis.csd.auth.gr/systems/dr-device.html.
[12] www.csd.uoc.gr/~bikakis/DR-Prolog/.

4. Four or five people can carry out this advanced project over the course of a term. The aim is to implement a proof layer in a multi-agent environment – that is, requests and proof parts will be exchanged between agents. Additional aspects to be considered include the following:

(a) Choose and familiarize yourselves with a multi-agent system. We have had good experience with JADE.[13]

(b) Represent proofs in an XML language, ideally by extending RuleML.

(c) Decide on the precise messages to be exchanged between agents.

---

[13]jade.tilab.com/.

Chapter 6

Applications

Recent years have seen a dramatic acceleration in the uptake of Semantic Web technologies, whereas the first years of Semantic Web applications (2000–2007) were mostly dominated by industrial or academic prototypes that did not go into full production. More recent years (since 2008) have seen full-scale production systems in a variety of sectors in business and commerce that have used Semantic Web technologies in an essential manner. In this chapter, we will briefly describe some of these applications.

Chapter Overview

We describe how deploying the GoodRelations ontology is beginning to change how the online retail sector functions (section 6.1), how the BBC has been exploiting Semantic Web technologies for maintaining and publishing their artists and music archives (section 6.2) as well as for their reporting on high profile sports events (section 6.3), how governments have been using semantic technologies for publishing their data (section 6.4), and how the publishing industry is using Semantic Web technology, using the New York Times as an example (section 6.5). Finally, we discuss the future of web search by briefly describing Sig.ma (section 6.6), OpenCalais (section 6.7), and Schema.org (section 6.8).

6.1   GoodRelations

6.1.1   Background

e-commerce, and in particular Business-to-Consumer (B2C) e-commerce, has been one of the main drivers behind the rapid adoption of the World Wide Web in everyday live. It is now commonplace to see URLs listed on storefronts and goods vehicles. Taking the UK as an example, the B2C market has grown from £87 million in April 2000 to £68.4 billion by the end of 2009, a thousand-fold increase over a single decade.

This large e-commerce marketplace is suffering from all the deficits of the traditional web: e-commerce websites are typically generated from structured information systems, listing price, availability, type of product, delivery options, etc., but by the time this information reaches the company's web pages, it has been turned into HTML and all machine-interpretable structure has disappeared, with the result that machines can no longer distinguish a price from a product-code. Search engines suffer from this inability to interpret the e-commerce pages that they try to crawl and index, and are unable to correctly distinguish product-types or to produce meaningful groupings of products.

GoodRelations[1] is an OWL-compliant ontology that describes the domain of electronic commerce. It can be used to express an offering of a product, to specify a price, to describe a business, and the like. The RDFa syntax for GoodRelations allows this information to be embedded into existing web pages so that they can be processed by other computers. The primary benefit of GoodRelations and the main driver behind its rapidly increasing adoption is how it improves search. Adding GoodRelations to web

---

[1]http://www.heppnetz.de/projects/goodrelations/.

pages improves the visibility of offers in modern search engines and recommender systems. GoodRelations allows for the annotation of products and services on the web in a way that can be used by search engines to deliver a better search experience to their users. It allows for very specific search queries and gives very precise answers.

Besides information on products and providers, the GoodRelations ontology also allows the expression of commercial and functional details of e-commerce transactions, such as eligible countries, payment and delivery options, quantity discounts, opening hours, etc.

The GoodRelations ontology[2] contains classes such as gr:ProductOrServiceModel, gr:PriceSpecification, gr:OpeningHoursSpecification and gr:DeliveryChargeSpecification, with properties such as gr:typeOfGood, gr:acceptedPaymentMethods, gr:hasCurrency and gr:eligibleRegions, among many others.

6.1.2   Example

We show a simple but realistic example taken from the pages of the Karneval Alarm shop, selling party costumes in Germany. A particular web page[3] describes a superman costume in size 48/50 for the price of 59.90 euros. This product (number 935 from Karneval Alarm's catalogue) is represented as the RDF entity offering_935 and, using the RDFa syntax, the web page for this product contains, among others, the following RDF statements:

```
offering_935 gr:name "Superman Kostum 48/50" ;
    gr:availableAtOrFrom http://www.karneval-alarm.de/#shop ;
    gr:hasPriceSpecification UnitPriceSpecification_935 .
UnitPriceSpecification_935 gr:hasCurrency "EUR" ;
                    gr:hasCurrencyValue "59.9" ;
                    gr:valueAddedTaxIncluded "true" .
```

[2]http://www.heppnetz.de/ontologies/goodrelations/v1.
[3]http://www.karneval-alarm.de/superman-m.html.

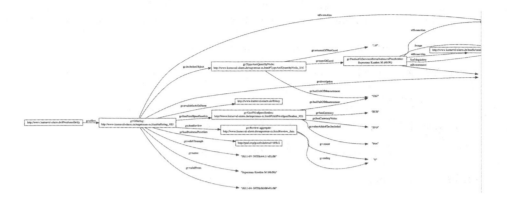

Figure 6.1: Triples extracted from RDFa markup in the product page for a superman costume

These descriptions can also be browsed online[4] using the RDFa inspector from Sindice.[5] See figure 6.1 for the overall graph, or use an online zoom-able view.[6]

Of course, such GoodRelation annotations need to mention product types and categories. For this purpose, the Product Ontology[7] describes products that are derived from Wikipedia pages.

An example would be

```
pto:Party_costume a owl:Class;
     rdfs:subClassOf gr:ProductOrService;
     rdfs:label "Party Costume"@en;
     rdfs:comment """A party costume is clothing..."""@en
```

which would allow us to say

```
offering_935 pr:typeOfGood pto:Party_Costume
```

The Product Ontology contains several hundred thousand OWL DL class definitions of products. These class definitions are tightly coupled with Wikipedia: the edits

---

[4]http://www.karneval-alarm.de/superman-m.html.

[5]http://inspector.sindice.com/.

[6]http://inspector.sindice.com/inspect?url=
http%3A//www.karneval-alarm.de/superman-m.html#GRAPH.

[7]http://www.productontology.org/.

in Wikipedia are reflected in the Product Ontology. This means that if a supplier sells a product that is not listed in the Product Ontology, they can create a page for it in Wikipedia and the product type will appear within 24 hours in the Product Ontology.

6.1.3   Adoption

The first company to adopt the GoodRelations ontology on a large scale was BestBuy, a large US retailer of consumer electronics. BestBuy reported a 30 percent increase in search traffic for its GoodRelation-enhanced pages, and a significantly increased click-through rate. Google is now recommending the use of GoodRelations for semantic markup of e-commerce pages, and both Yahoo and Google are crawling RDFa statements and using them to enhance the presentation of their search results. Other adopters at the time of writing are Overstock.com retailers, the O'Reilly Media publishing house, the Peek & Cloppenburg clothing chain store, and smaller enterprises such as Robinson Outdoors and the aforementioned Karneval Alarm. At the time of writing, the Sindice semantic search engine lists 273,000 pages annotated with the GoodRelations vocabulary.

6.1.4   Publication

Martin Hepp. GoodRelations: An Ontology for Describing Products and Services Offers on the Web. In Proceedings of the 16th International Conference on Knowledge Engineering and Knowledge Management (EKAW2008). Acitrezza, Italy. September 29 – October 3, 2008. Springer LNCS, Vol 5268, 332–347.

6.2 BBC Artists

6.2.1 Background

The BBC Music Beta project[8] is an effort by the BBC to build semantically linked and annotated web pages about artists and singers whose songs are played on BBC radio stations. Within these pages, collections of data are enhanced and interconnected with semantic metadata, letting music fans explore connections between artists that they may have not known existed.

Previously, writers at the BBC would have to write (and keep up to date) interesting and relevant content on every single artist page they published. Instead, on the Music Beta project, the BBC is pulling in information from external sites such as MusicBrainz and Wikipedia and aggregating this information to build their web pages.

For this purpose, the BBC has adopted the RDF standard, and has mapped its own data schema with that published by MusicBrainz to utilize the unique identifiers that MusicBrainz provides. This allows the BBC site to leverage public domain content, augmenting the profile pages found there. MusicBrainz is an open content music "metadatabase" that lists information for over 400,000 artists; the information contained in the info-boxes on Wikipedia pages is captured in DBPedia.

6.2.2 Example

As an example, we can look at the BBC Artist web page for John Lennon.[9] At first sight, this web page looks like a regular web page with artist information such as biographical information, professional information such as artists that John Lennon played with and the bands he played in, reviews of albums, etc. But the page is also a rich set of RDF triples, using the MusicBrainz identifier for John Lennon 4d5447d7 as a resource to state such information as:

---

[8]http://www.bbc.co.uk/music/artists.
[9]http://www.bbc.co.uk/music/artists/4d5447d7-c61c-4120-ba1b-d7f471d385b9.

```
5c014631#artist foaf:name "John Lennon"
```

```
4d5447d7#artist bio:event _:node15vknin3hx2
_:node15vknin3hx2 rdf:type bio:Death
_:node15vknin3hx2 bio:date "1980-12-08"
```

```
4d5447d7#artist foaf:made _:node15vknin3hx7
_:node15vknin3hx7 dc:title "John Lennon/Plastic Ono Band"
4d5447d7#artist owl:sameAs dbpedia:John_Lennon
```

which states that the artist named John Lennon died on December 12, 1980, that he made a record entitled "John Lennon/Plastic Ono Band," and that he is also known under the URI dbpedia:John_Lennon.

The full content of the BBC Artist page on John Lennon contains 60 triples, from which a further 300 triples can be inferred using 40 different ontologies describing family relations, the music domain, times and dates, geographical information, social relations, and others.

The full site has in the order of 400,000 artist pages, 160,000 external links and 100,000 artist-to-artist relationships.

The use of Semantic Web technology, such as using URIs as identifiers and aligning these with external semantic data providers, means web pages can be created and maintained with a fraction of the manpower required in the past. It is interesting to note that the BBC is not only consuming such information resources, but is also serving them back to the world. Simply adding .rdf to the URI of any BBC Artist web page will actually serve the RDF on which the page is based. By publishing the RDF in this manner, the BBC is making their data available to third parties wanting to use it elsewhere.

Of course, when using public information as input, there is always the risk of such information containing errors. In such cases, the BBC does not repair those errors internally. Instead, they will repair the errors on the external sources such as MusicBrainz and DBPedia. This not only results in repairing the errors on the BBC site as well (since it is feeding of those sources), but it also repairs the error for any other user of these data sources, thereby contributing to increased quality of publicly available data sources.

6.2.3   Adoption

The BBC Artist project is "a part of a general movement that's going on at the BBC to move away from pages that are built in a variety of legacy content production systems to actually publishing data that we can use in a more dynamic way across the web." The BBC is basing other parts of their website on Linked Data standards and resources including program information,[10] with URI's for programs and using the BBC's program ontology,[11] and wildlife information from the BBC's extensive range of high-quality nature programs using the BBC's own WildLife ontology.[12]

6.3   BBC World Cup 2010 Website

6.3.1   Background

Besides broadcasting radio and television programs, the BBC puts substantial effort into building websites to provide news and media information. For their website for the 2010 World Cup soccer event, the BBC deployed semantic technologies in order to achieve more automatic content publishing, a higher number of pages manageable with a lower headcount, semantic navigation, and personalization.

---

[10]http://www.bbc.co.uk/programmes.
[11]http://www.bbc.co.uk/ontologies/programmes/2009-09-07.shtml.
[12]http://www.bbc.co.uk/ontologies/wildlife/2010-02-22.shtml.

6.3.2   Example

A typical page for a player looks like the one in figure 6.2.[13] Similar pages exist for hundreds of players, dozens of teams, all groups, all matches, etc., and of course all of these are highly interlinked.

The BBC has developed small ontologies to capture the domain of soccer, including domain-specific notions concerning soccer teams and tournaments, as well as very generic notions for events and geographic locations, using well-known ontologies such as FOAF[14] and GeoNames.[15]

Figure 6.3 shows a small example of the BBC's World Cup ontology. These ontologies were used to infer additional information for display to the user, such as which national competition a player participates in and which team the player is a member of.

6.3.3   Adoption

The system powering the BBC World Cup site has a classical three-tier architecture, with (i) all information stored in an RDF triple-store, (ii) this triple store organized by a number of ontologies that enable querying of the triple store, and (iii) a user-interface layer that uses ontology-based queries to the triple store to obtain information to display to the user.

With this publishing model, the BBC claims to have greatly increased their opportunities for content reuse and repurposing, reduced the journalist headcount required to maintain the site, and improved the user experience through semantically driven page-layout and multi-dimensional entry-points (player, match, group, etc.).

At its peak, the system was powered by a commercial triple-store vendor that was handling a thousand SPARQL queries per minute (amounting to over a million queries a day), together with hundreds of RDF statements inserted or updated every minute, as

---

[13]http://news.bbc.co.uk/sport/football/world_cup_2010/groups_and_teams/team/england/wayne_rooney.

[14]http://xmlns.com/foaf/spec/.

[15]http://www.geonames.org/.

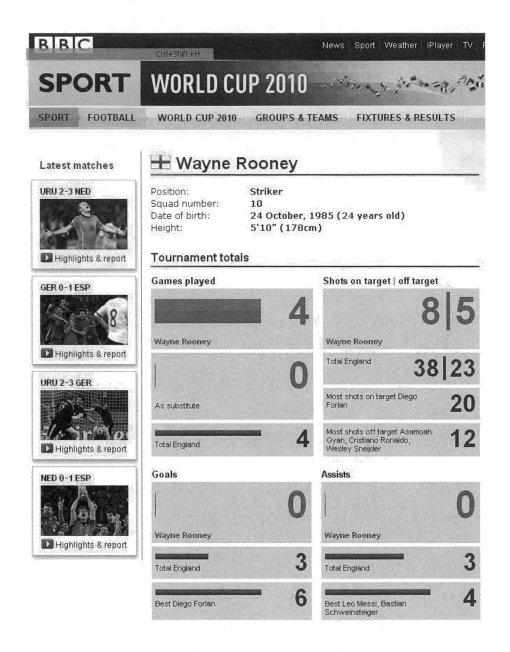

Figure 6.2: Typical page from BBC World Cup website

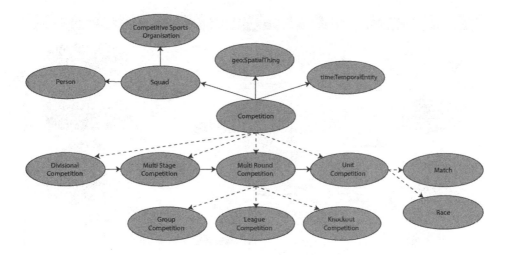

Figure 6.3: Part of the BBC's sports tournament ontology

well as using full OWL inference.

The BBC is planning to adopt the same approach to their Olympics 2012 website, which will have to cover over 10,000 athletes from over 200 countries, with pages for every discipline and for every event, displaying near real-time statistics and serving 58,000 hours of video content. Figure 6.4 shows a small part of the general sports ontology that the BBC is developing.

6.4 Government Data

6.4.1 Background

Some of the early large-scale adoption of Semantic Web technologies in the world was a result of the Obama administration's drive towards more transparency of government. Publishing data sources that had traditionally been locked up inside governmental institutions and not available to the public was seen as a crucial step toward more transparent government, and Semantic Web technologies were seen as a key technology for publishing these data. Sites such as http://data.gov have by now published some

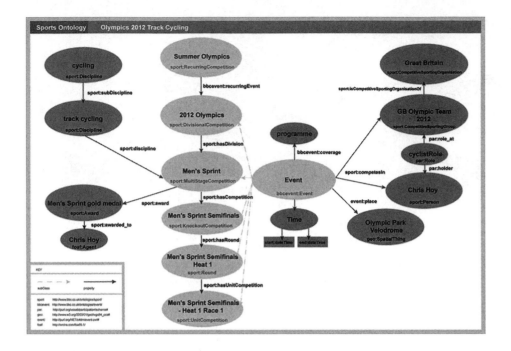

Figure 6.4: Part of the BBC's Olympics ontology

250,000 datasets from 250 different government agencies, ranging from economic indicators to health-service statistics, and even environmental data. Not all (or even: not much) of this data is in full Linked Data format, exploiting RDF, URIs, ontologies, and linking to other datasets. In this context, it is useful to consider the *5-star* scale introduced by the W3C as a road toward publishing Linked Data that starts with much simpler technologies. In brief:

⋆ *put data on the web at all, in any format, anywhere.* For example, just putting PDF documents with tables (or even scanned documents) on a website somewhere would already rate as a 1-⋆ step in publishing data. Although technically trivial, in practice this already means overcoming social, organizational, and bureaucratic hurdles.

⋆⋆ *use a machine readable format.* This means avoiding formats such as PDF documents. Publishing Excel spreadsheets is the most typical example of a 2-⋆ data-publishing step.

⋆ ⋆ ⋆ *use an open format.* This means avoiding propriety formats such as Excel, and instead using open formats like .csv file or Open Office format. Typically simple format-transformation steps might suffice to get from a 2-⋆ to a 3-⋆ rating.

⋆ ⋆ ⋆⋆ *give a URL for each data item.* This is the first step where web semantics is making its appearance: use a URI to denote every data-type, data-item, and data-property. This allows others to link to the published dataset.

⋆ ⋆ ⋆ ⋆ ⋆ Finally, *link out to shared vocabularies.* For example, use the DBPedia term for city when talking about the class of all cities, and similar terms for names of entities and properties. This use of external vocabularies truly enables the interlinking of datasets across different sites.

6.4.2 Adoption

Although much of the data on http://data.gov has been (and still is) only in 2-⋆ format, it turned out not to be hard to move this data up in the above ranking system. In a period of eight months, students at the Rensselaer Polytechnic Institute managed to "web-enable" 6.4 billion data-items from http://data.gov, and (more significantly), they created applications for such diverse projects as plotting postal service expenditure against performance, plotting wilderness fires against agency budgets (to measure effectiveness), covering interstate migration from information on tax forms, plotting family income against Medicare claims, comparing agency budgets across three public budget datasets, and plotting social networks of people visiting the White House. Although impossible to establish a causal link, the number of citizen appeals under the Freedom of Information Act have reportedly dropped substantially since the launch of http://data.gov.

Encouraged by this success, other governments have started to follow this example, including the governments of many states and large cities in the US, countries like Canada, Ireland, Norway, Australia, and New Zealand, and citizen-initiatives have started in countries such as France, Italy, Denmark, Austria, Germany, and many others. Perhaps the most significant take-up has been in the UK, where http://data.gov.uk has received strong support from the government, and where it is seen as not only a step towards more transparent government, but also a cost-reduction mechanism. Instead of building and maintaining expensive websites with governmental information, the government simply publishes the underlying data sources and encourages third parties (be it either citizens or commercial parties) to develop services on top of these published data sources. In the US alone, over 200 applications built by third parties have been reported. Such notable applications from around the world include a safety map of bicycle routes, information for home buyers about their new neighborhoods, a school finder, a nursery finder, pollution alerts, a regional expenditure map, and WhereDidMyTaxGo.[16]

Finally, intergovernmental agencies are following the same path, such as the World Bank (data.worldbank.org), the European Commission's website for European tendering procedures (ted.europa.eu), and the European statistics office Eurostat (ec.europa.eu/eurostat/).

6.5 *New York Times*

Since 1913, the *New York Times* has been maintaining an index of all subjects on which it has published. This has grown into a collection of almost 30,000 "subject headings," describing locations, people, organizations, and events. Every article in the *New York Times* since its first appearance in 1851 has been tagged with these subject headings, and such tags are being used to provide news-alerting services, to automate the editorial process, and to build "topic pages" that collect all *New York Times* information for a

---
[16]http://www.wheredidmytaxgo.co.uk/.

given topic.

In 2009, the *New York Times* started to convert its entire subject headings index to Semantic Web format. Not only is the entire headings list being published in RDF format, but the terms are also being linked to hubs on the Linked Data Web such as DBPedia, Freebase, and GeoNames. By 2010, this process was finished for about 30 percent of all subject headings.

The *New York Times* has reported that the linking of their subject headings with the Linked Data Web helps them to provide geographic information (through the link with GeoNames), helps them to align articles with other data sources that are often used by the newspaper, such as the Library of Congress, and makes it possible to rapidly build nonstandard mash-ups of their archive material, such as finding all items about the alumni of a given University.

6.6   Sig.ma and Sindice

Whereas applications such as GoodRelations help traditional search engines to improve their results without ever confronting the end-user with the underlying RDF graphs, the search engine Sindice[17] and its front-end Sig.ma[18] are different: Sindice operates directly on the RDF graph that makes up the global Semantic Web, and Sig.ma presents to the user the binary relations that are discovered in this way.

Sindice has a classical search engine architecture: a crawler, a very large indexed store, and a retrieval interface. But the difference from a classical search engine is that Sindice does not retrieve and index words and phrases, but instead retrieves and indexes RDF graphs. At the time of writing, Sindice indexes some 400 million RDF "documents," resulting in 12 billion RDF statements. These statements are indexed and available for querying through a SPARQL endpoint. This produces a database-like

---

[17] http://sindice.com.
[18] http://sigm.ma.

access to the Web of Data that can be used by developers and businesses to power products and services. Interestingly, the Sindice crawler is not limited to crawling RDF-graphs but also crawls other forms of structured data, such as those using the HTML5 microdata format using the schema.org vocabulary, or other microformats.

Sig.ma is a user interface that was created as a demonstration of live querying on the Web of Data. Starting from keyword search, Sig.ma identifies the URLs on the Web of Data that are relevant to a keyword and finds all triples that describe these URLs. Through an interactive user interface the user can investigate which triples originate from which data sources, select or remove specific data sources, "walk the graph" by clicking on the URLs which are given as related to the search term, and turn on the URLs related to those, etc.

By using the Sindice search engine, Sig.ma gives the user a live view of what is on the "Web of Data" about any given topic. Due to its ingenious user interface and to the very complete database of Sindice, Sig.ma is probably the best location for lay users to get a feel for the structure and size of the current Web of Data and the sheer amount of knowledge it already captures.

6.7   OpenCalais

The press agency Thompson Reuters produces thousands of news items every day, covering wide areas of science, business, politics, and sports. Although originally intended to be read by humans, a key observation of Reuters is that many of the consumers of their news items are no longer people, but instead computers. Computers are reading the news flowing out of Reuters, analyzing it and producing summaries, reading lists, financial investment advice, etc.

This leads to the paradoxical situation of computers producing information for computers using unstructured natural language as a rather unsuited communication medium. Reuter's OpenCalais service is intended to help computers process data cap-

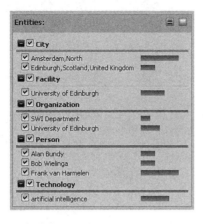

Figure 6.5: Objects and relations recognized by OpenCalais

tured in natural language texts. It does this by analyzing a text, recognizing named entities such as people, locations, companies, etc., and annotating the text with RDF to identify these named entities.

As a simple example, the following text produces the entities and relations as shown in figure 6.5:

> After studying mathematics and computer science in Amsterdam, Frank van Harmelen moved to the Department of AI of the University of Edinburgh. While in Edinburgh, he worked with Prof. Alan Bundy on proof planning for inductive theorem proving. After his PhD research, he moved back to Amsterdam where he worked from 1990 to 1995 in the SWI Department under Prof. Bob Wielinga. In 1995 he joined the AI research group at the Vrije Universiteit Amsterdam.

For these objects, Reuters uses its own URIs to identify the entities, but many of these private URIs are linked through owl:sameAs statements to more widely adopted URIs for the same entities taken from GeoNames, DBPedia, FreeBase, the Internet Movie Database, and others. This allows us to further retrieve information about these entities from Reuter's database, such as financial information, names of board members, etc. Thus, through OpenCalais, it is possible to move from a natural language text mentioning a term to a web of structured information items. In 2011, Calais was reported to be processing five million documents per day.

6.8   Schema.org

Schema.org is an effort by search engine providers (Google, Yahoo, Microsoft, Yandex) to encourage the semantic mark up of pages. It encourages this through the definition of a common schema or vocabulary available at schema.org. The vocabulary covers common things that people search for, such as products, jobs, and events. By using a common vocabulary, search engines are able to better index pages but also show richer information in search results.

Schema.org supports markup presented both in microdata and RDFa 1.1 Lite. Thus, one can mix the Schema.org vocabulary with others on the web such as the previously discussed Good-Relations ontology. Schema.org shows how applications can drive the adoption of machine-understandable markup.

6.9   Summary

Semantic Web technologies are being used in a wide variety of applications, from powering websites to making it easier for search engines to understand the content of web pages. A key idea in all of these applications is that common ontologies provide a basis for integrating and understanding knowledge from multiple sources. We have highlighted only some major Semantic Web applications, though there are countless more that are being used everyday. We encourage you to investigate and see what else is being done.

Chapter 7

Ontology Engineering

7.1 Introduction

So far, we have focused mainly on the techniques that are essential to the Semantic Web: representation languages, query languages, transformation and inference techniques, and tools. Clearly, the introduction of such a large volume of new tools and techniques also raises methodological questions: How can tools and techniques best be applied? Which languages and tools should be used in which circumstances, and in which order? What about issues of quality control and resource management?

Chapter Overview

Many of these questions for the Semantic Web have been studied in other contexts – for example, in software engineering, object-oriented design, and knowledge engineering. It is beyond the scope of this book to give a comprehensive treatment of all of these issues. Nevertheless, in this chapter, we briefly discuss some of the methodological issues that arise when building ontologies, in particular, constructing ontologies manually (section 7.2), reusing ontologies (section 7.3), and using semiautomatic methods (section 7.4). Section 7.5 discusses ontology mapping. Section 7.6 describes how to populate ontology instances from relational databases. Finally, section 7.7 explains how Semantic Web tools can be integrated into a single architecture to build applications.

7.2   Constructing Ontologies Manually

For our discussion of the manual construction of ontologies, we follow mainly Noy and McGuinness, "Ontology Development 101: A Guide to Creating Your First Ontology." Further references are provided in suggested reading.

We can distinguish the following main stages in the ontology development process:

1. Determine scope.
2. Consider reuse.
3. Enumerate terms.
4. Define taxonomy.
5. Define properties.
6. Define facets.
7. Define instances.
8. Check for anomalies.

Like any development process, this is in practice not linear. These steps will have to be iterated, and backtracking to earlier steps may be necessary at any point in the process. We will not further discuss this complex process management. Instead, we turn to the individual steps.

7.2.1   Determine Scope

Developing an ontology of a domain is not a goal in itself. Developing an ontology is akin to defining a set of data and its structure for other programs to use. In other words, an ontology is a *model* of a particular domain, built for a particular purpose. As a consequence, there is no *correct* ontology of a specific domain. An ontology is by necessity an abstraction of a particular domain, and there are always viable alternatives. What is included in this abstraction should be determined by the use to which the ontology will be put, and by future extensions that are already anticipated. Basic questions to be answered at this stage are: What is the domain that the ontology will cover? For what we are going to use the ontology? For what types of questions should the ontology provide answers? Who will use and maintain the ontology?

7.2.2 Consider Reuse

With the spreading deployment of the Semantic Web, many ontologies, especially for common domains (social networks, medicine, geography), are available for use. Thus, we rarely have to start from scratch when defining an ontology. There is almost always an ontology available from a third party that provides at least a useful starting point for our own ontology (see section 7.3).

7.2.3 Enumerate Terms

A first step toward the actual definition of the ontology is to write down in an unstructured list all the relevant terms that are expected to appear in the ontology. Typically, nouns form the basis for class names, and verbs (or verb phrases) form the basis for property names (e.g., *is part of*, *has component*).

Traditional knowledge engineering tools such as laddering and grid analysis can be productively used at this stage to obtain both the set of terms and an initial structure for these terms.

7.2.4 Define Taxonomy

After the identification of relevant terms, these terms must be organized in a taxonomic hierarchy. Opinions differ on whether it is more efficient/reliable to do this in a top-down or a bottom-up fashion.

It is, of course, important to ensure that the hierarchy is indeed a taxonomic (subclass) hierarchy. In other words, if A is a subclass of B, then every instance of A must also be an instance of B. Only this will ensure that we respect the built-in semantics of primitives such as rdfs:subClassOf.

7.2.5 Define Properties

This step is often interleaved with the previous one: it is natural to organize the properties that link the classes while organizing these classes in a hierarchy.

Remember that the semantics of the subClassOf relation demands that whenever A is a subclass of B, every property statement that holds for instances of B must also apply to instances of A. Because of this inheritance, it makes sense to attach properties to the highest class in the hierarchy to which they apply.

While attaching properties to classes, it also makes sense to immediately provide statements about the domain and range of these properties. There is a methodological tension here between generality and specificity. On the one hand, it is attractive to give properties as general a domain and range as possible, enabling the properties to be used (through inheritance) by subclasses. On the other hand, it is useful to define domain and range as narrowly as possible, enabling us to detect potential inconsistencies and misconceptions in the ontology by spotting domain and range violations.

7.2.6 Define Facets

It is interesting to note that after all these steps, the ontology will only require the expressivity provided by RDF Schema and does not use any of the additional primitives in OWL. This will change in the current step, which is enriching the previously defined properties with facets:

- Cardinality. Specify for as many properties as possible whether they are allowed or required to have a certain number of different values. Often, occurring cases are "at least one value" (i.e., required properties) and "at most one value" (i.e., single-valued properties).

- Required values. Often, classes are defined by virtue of a certain property's having particular values, and such required values can be specified in OWL, using owl:hasValue. Sometimes the requirements are less stringent: a property is required to have some values from a given class (and not necessarily a specific value, i.e., owl:someValuesFrom).

- Relational characteristics. The final family of facets concerns the relational characteristics of properties: symmetry, transitivity, inverse properties, and functional values.

After this step in the ontology construction process, it will be possible to check the ontology for internal inconsistencies. (This is not possible before this step, simply because RDF Schema is not rich enough to express inconsistencies.) Examples of often occurring inconsistencies are incompatible domain and range definitions for transitive, symmetric, or inverse properties. Similarly, cardinality properties are frequent sources of inconsistencies. Finally, requirements on property values can conflict with domain and range restrictions, giving yet another source of possible inconsistencies.

7.2.7   Define Instances

Of course, we rarely define ontologies for their own sake. Instead we use ontologies to organize sets of instances, and it is a separate step to fill the ontologies with such intances. Typically, the number of instances is many orders of magnitude larger than the number of classes from the ontology. Ontologies vary in size from a few hundred classes to tens of thousands of classes; the number of instances varies from hundreds to hundreds of thousands, or even larger.

Because of these large numbers, populating an ontology with instances is typically not done manually. Often, instances are retrieved from legacy data sources such as databases as discussed in Section 7.6. Another often used technique is the automated extraction of instances from a text corpus.

7.2.8   Check for Anomalies

An important advantage of using OWL rather than RDF Schema is the possibility of detecting inconsistencies in the ontology itself, or in the set of instances that were defined to populate the ontology. Examples of often occurring anomalies are incompatible domain and range definitions for transitive, symmetric, or inverse properties. Similarly, cardinality properties are frequent sources of inconsistencies. Finally, the requirements on property values can conflict with domain and range restrictions, giving yet another source of possible inconsistencies.

7.3   Reusing Existing Ontologies

One should begin with an existing ontology if possible. Existing ontologies come in a wide variety.

7.3.1   Codified Bodies of Expert Knowledge

Some ontologies are carefully crafted by a large team of experts over many years. An example in the medical domain is the cancer ontology from the National Cancer Institute in the United States.[1] Examples in the cultural domain are the Art and Architecture Thesaurus (AAT),[2] containing 125,000 terms, and the Union List of Artist Names (ULAN),[3] with 220,000 entries on artists. Another example is the Iconclass vocabulary of 28,000 terms for describing cultural images.[4] An example from the geographical domain is the Getty Thesaurus of Geographic Names (TGN),[5] containing over 1 million entries.

---

[1] www.mindswap.org/2003/CancerOntology/.
[2] www.getty.edu/research/tools/vocabulary/aat.
[3] www.getty.edu/research/conducting_research/vocabularies/ulan.
[4] www.iconclass.nl/.
[5] www.getty.edu/research/conducting_research/vocabularies/tgn.

7.3.2 Integrated Vocabularies

Sometimes attempts have been made to merge a number of independently developed vocabularies into a single large resource. The prime example of this is the Unified Medical Language System,[6] which integrates 100 biomedical vocabularies and classifications. The UMLS metathesaurus alone contains 750,000 concepts, with over 10 million links between them. Not surprisingly, the semantics of such a resource that integrates many independently developed vocabularies is rather low, but nevertheless it has turned out to be very useful in many applications, at least as a starting point.

7.3.3 Upper-Level Ontologies

Whereas the preceding ontologies are all highly domain-specific, some attempts have been made to define very generally applicable ontologies (sometimes known as upper-level ontologies). The two prime examples are Cyc,[7] with 60,000 assertions on 6,000 concepts, and the Standard Upperlevel Ontology (SUO).[8]

7.3.4 Topic Hierarchies

Other "ontologies" hardly deserve this name in a strict sense: they are simply sets of terms, loosely organized in a specialization hierarchy. This hierarchy is typically not a strict taxonomy but rather mixes different specialization relations, such as *is-a, part-of,* or *contained-in*. Nevertheless, such resources are often very useful as a starting point. A large example is the Open Directory hierarchy,[9] which contains more than 400,000 hierarchically organized categories and is available in RDF format.

---

[6]umlsinfo.nlm.nih.gov/.
[7]www.opencyc.org/.
[8]suo.ieee.org/.
[9]dmoz.org/.

7.3.5   Linguistic Resources

Some resources were originally built not as abstractions of a particular domain but rather as linguistic resources. Again, these have been shown to be useful as starting places for ontology development. The prime example in this category is WordNet, with over 90,000 word sense definitions.[10]

7.3.6   Encyclopedic Knowledge

Wikipedia, the community-generated encyclopedia, provides a plethora of information about a range of topics. The DBpedia project[11] extracts knowledge from Wikipedia and exposes it as Linked Data using RDF and OWL. The breadth of knowledge from Wikipedia has made the site a first point of reference when building ontologies. Yago[12] is another knowledge base that leverages Wikipedia but it also contains information from Wordnet and geographical resources like GeoNames.[13]

7.3.7   Ontology Libraries

There are several online repositories of ontologies. Examples include the TONES ontology repository,[14] the BioPortal,[15] and those provided with the Protégé ontology editor.[16] Perhaps the best current repository of online ontologies is Swoogle,[17] which has cataloged over 10,000 Semantic Web documents and indexed metadata about their classes, properties, and individuals as well as the relationships among them. Swoogle also defines a ranking property for Semantic Web documents and uses this to help sort search results. Alternatively, the Sindice search index maintains an index of almost all

---

[10] http://wordnet.princeton.edu/, available in RDF at http://semanticweb.cs.vu.nl/lod/wn30/.
[11] http://dbpedia.org.
[12] http://www.mpi-inf.mpg.de/yago-naga/yago/.
[13] http://www.geonames.org/.
[14] http://owl.cs.manchester.ac.uk/repository/browser.
[15] See http://bioportal.bioontology.org/.
[16] Reachable from http://protege.stanford.edu/download/ontologies.html.
[17] http://swoogle.umbc.edu/.

RDF data published on the Semantic Web.[18] Prefix.cc[19] lists the most commonly used namespace prefixes used on the Semantic Web. These prefixes link to the corresponding ontology they represent.

It is only rarely the case that existing ontologies can be reused without changes. Typically, existing concepts and properties must be refined (using owl:subClassOf and owl:subPropertyOf). Also, alternative names must be introduced which are better suited to the particular domain (e.g., using owl:equivalentClass and owl:equivalentProperty). Also, this is an opportunity for fruitfully exploiting the fact that RDF and OWL allow private refinements of classes defined in other ontologies.

The general question of importing ontologies and establishing mappings between them is still wide open, and is considered to be one of the hardest Semantic Web research issues.

7.4   Semiautomatic Ontology Acquisition

There are two core challenges for putting the vision of the Semantic Web into action.

First, one has to support the reengineering task of semantic enrichment for building the web of metadata. The success of the Semantic Web greatly depends on the proliferation of ontologies and relational metadata. This requires that such metadata can be produced at high speed and low cost. To this end, the task of merging and aligning ontologies for establishing semantic interoperability may be supported by machine learning techniques.

Second, one has to provide a means for maintaining and adopting the machine-processable data that are the basis for the Semantic Web. Thus, we need mechanisms that support the dynamic nature of the web.

Although ontology engineering tools have matured over the last decade, manual

---

[18]http://sindice.com.
[19]http://prefix.cc.

ontology acquisition remains a time-consuming, expensive, highly skilled, and sometimes cumbersome task that can easily result in a knowledge acquisition bottleneck.

These problems resemble those that knowledge engineers have dealt with over the last two decades as they worked on knowledge acquisition methodologies or workbenches for defining knowledge bases. The integration of knowledge acquisition with machine learning techniques proved beneficial for knowledge acquisition.

The research area of machine learning has a long history, both on knowledge acquisition or extraction and on knowledge revision or maintenance, and it provides a large number of techniques that may be applied to solve these challenges. The following tasks can be supported by machine learning techniques:

- Extraction of ontologies from existing data on the web

- Extraction of relational data and metadata from existing data on the web

- Merging and mapping ontologies by analyzing extensions of concepts

- Maintaining ontologies by analyzing instance data

- Improving Semantic Web applications by observing users

Machine learning provides a number of techniques that can be used to support these tasks:

- Clustering

- Incremental ontology updates

- Support for the knowledge engineer

- Improving large natural language ontologies

- Pure (domain) ontology learning

Omelayenko (see suggested readings) identifies the following three types of ontologies that can be supported using machine learning techniques.

7.4.1   Natural Language Ontologies

Natural language ontologies (NLOs) contain lexical relations between language concepts; they are large in size and do not require frequent updates. Usually they represent the background knowledge of the system and are used to expand user queries. The state of the art in NLO learning looks quite optimistic: not only does a stable general-purpose NLO exist but so do techniques for automatically or semiautomatically constructing and enriching domain-specific NLOs.

7.4.2   Domain Ontologies

Domain ontologies capture knowledge of one particular domain, such as pharmacological or printer knowledge. These ontologies provide a detailed description of the domain concepts in a restricted domain. Usually, they are constructed manually, but different learning techniques can assist the (especially the inexperienced) knowledge engineer. Learning domain ontologies is far less developed than NLO improvement. The acquisition of domain ontologies is still guided by a human knowledge engineer, and automated learning techniques play a minor role in knowledge acquisition. They have to find statistically valid dependencies in the domain texts and suggest them to the knowledge engineer.

7.4.3   Ontology Instances

Ontology instances can be generated automatically and frequently updated (e.g., a company profile in the Yellow Pages will be updated frequently) while the ontology remains unchanged. The task of learning of the ontology instances fits nicely into a machine learning framework, and there are several successful applications of machine learning algorithms for this. But these applications are either strictly dependent on the domain ontology or populate the markup without relating to any domain theory. A general-purpose technique for extracting ontology instances from texts given the domain ontology as input has still not been developed.

Besides the different types of ontologies that can be supported, there are also different uses for ontology learning. The first three tasks in the following list (again, taken from Omelayenko) relate to ontology acquisition tasks in knowledge engineering, and the last three to ontology maintenance tasks:

- Ontology creation from scratch by the knowledge engineer. In this task machine learning assists the knowledge engineer by suggesting the most important relations in the field or checking and verifying the constructed knowledge bases.

- Ontology schema extraction from web documents. In this task machine learning systems take the data and metaknowledge (like a metaontology) as input and generate the ready-to-use ontology as output with the possible help of the knowledge engineer.

- Extraction of ontology instances populates given ontology schemas and extracts the instances of the ontology presented in the web documents. This task is similar to information extraction and page annotation, and can apply the techniques developed in these areas.

- Ontology integration and navigation deal with reconstructing and navigating in large and possibly machine-learned knowledge bases. For example, the task can be to change the propositional-level knowledge base of the machine learner into a first-order knowledge base.

- An ontology maintenance task is updating some parts of an ontology that are designed to be updated (like formatting tags that have to track the changes made in the page layout).

- Ontology enrichment (or ontology tuning) includes automated modification of minor relations into an existing ontology. This does not change major concepts and structures but makes an ontology more precise.

A wide variety of techniques, algorithms, and tools is available from machine learning. However, an important requirement for ontology representation is that ontologies must be symbolic, human-readable, and understandable. This forces us to deal only with symbolic learning algorithms that make generalizations and to skip other methods like neural networks and genetic algorithms. The following are some potentially applicable algorithms:

- Propositional rule learning algorithms learn association rules or other forms of attribute-value rules.

- Bayesian learning is mostly represented by the Naive Bayes classifier. It is based on the Bayes theorem and generates probabilistic attribute-value rules based on the assumption of conditional independence between the attributes of the training instances.

- First-order logic rules learning induces the rules that contain variables, called first-order Horn clauses.

- Clustering algorithms group the instances together based on the similarity or distance measures between a pair of instances defined in terms of their attribute values.

In conclusion, we can say that although there is much potential for machine learning techniques to be deployed for Semantic Web engineering, this is far from a well-understood area.

7.5   Ontology Mapping

With reuse rather than development-from-scratch becoming the norm for ontology deployment, ontology integration is an increasingly urgent task. It will rarely be the case that a single ontology fulfills the needs of a particular application; more often than not, multiple ontologies will have to be combined. This raises the problem of ontology integration (also called ontology alignment or ontology mapping). Because of its crucial nature, this problem has received wide attention in the research community in recent years.

Current approaches to ontology mapping deploy a whole host of different methods, coming from very different areas. We distinguish linguistic, statistical, structural, and logical methods.

7.5.1 Linguistic Methods

The most basic methods try to exploit the linguistic labels attached to the concepts in source and target ontology in order to discover potential matches. This can be as simple as basic stemming techniques or calculating Hamming distances, or it can use specialized domain knowledge. An example of the latter would be that the difference between *Diabetes Melitus type I* and *Diabetes Melitus type II* is not a negligible difference to be removed by a small Hamming distance.

7.5.2 Statistical Methods

Instead of using the linguistic labels of concepts, other methods use *instance data* to determine correspondences between concepts. If there is a significant statistical correlation between the instances of a source concept and a target concept, there is reason to believe that these concepts are strongly related (by a subsumption relation or perhaps even an equivalence relation). These approaches of course rely on the availability of a sufficiently large corpus of instances that are classified in both the source and the target ontologies.

7.5.3 Structural Methods

Since ontologies have internal structure, it makes sense to exploit the graph structure of the source and target ontologies and try to determine similarities between these structures, often in coordination with some of the other methods. If a source concept and a target concept have similar linguistic labels, then the dissimilarity of their graph neighborhoods could be used to detect homonym problems where purely linguistic methods would falsely declare a potential mapping.

7.5.4 Logical Methods

The methods that are perhaps most specific to mapping *ontologies* are the logical methods. After all, ontologies are, as defined by R. Studer, "*formal specifications* of a shared conceptualization," and it makes sense to exploit this formalization of both source and target structures. A serious limitation of this approach is that many practical ontologies are semantically rather lightweight and thus do not carry much logical formalism with them.

7.5.5 Mapping Implementations

There are several frameworks for ontology mapping such as the R2R Framework[20] and LIMES.[21] The service sameas.org collects and exposes owl:sameAs mappings from several different sources. While these projects have made great strides in creating mappings, this is still a challenging area. The research community has run the Ontology Alignment Evaluation Initiative[22] for the past nine years to encourage the creation of more accurate and comprehensive mappings.

---

[20] http://www4.wiwiss.fu-berlin.de/bizer/r2r/.
[21] http://aksw.org/Projects/LIMES?v=z1l.
[22] See http://oaei.ontologymatching.org/.

7.6   Exposing Relational Databases

Most websites today are not a series of static pages stored on a web server but are instead dynamically generated from data stored in *relational databases*. For example, a real estate website would maintain a database of various homes and apartments with information about price, location, and amenities. This database would then be used to populate web pages. Because so much data is available in relational databases, it can provide a convenient source of instance data.

Here, we give an overview of the process of exposing relational databases as ontologies.

7.6.1   Mapping Terminology

First, we revisit the terminology of a database and how the terminology can be mapped to RDFS/OWL terms. Below is an example *table* from a real estate database. A table is also called a *relation*. The table consist of series of columns with the headings HomeId, City, and Price. These columns are called *attributes*. Each of the rows of the table is called a *tuple*.

Homes

HomeId	City	Price (Euros)
1	Amsterdam	100 000
2	Utrecht	200 000

Based on this terminology, one can follow a simple approach to map the relational database schema to RDFS or OWL. Each table in the database can be considered a class. Each attribute can be considered a property and each tuple can be considered an instance. Thus, in our example, we have two instances of the class Home. Each instance has a property city and price and the corresponding values (e.g., for HomeId 1, the value of the city property is Amsterdam).

When performing a mapping one must also create URIs for each of the entities. This can often be done by prepending a namespace to the beginning of the attribute or table name. Likewise, one can often use the *primary key* for the URIs of each instance. It is important to note that a main difference between relational databases and RDF is that RDF uses URIs to identify entities, which means that everything has a globally unique identifier. Relational databases, however, have identifiers that are unique only within the local scope of the given database.

7.6.2   Conversion Tools

Because of the systematic mechanism by which relational databases can be mapped to ontologies, it is possible to automate much of the conversion process. There are several tools available, as identified by the W3C Relational Database to RDF Incubator Group report on approaches to mapping relational databases to RDF. You can find a link to the report in the suggested reading. Most of these tools work by analyzing the structure of the relational database and then generating almost complete RDF. The user is then required to modify configuration files in order to specify more appropriate URIs as well as link to existing ontologies. For example, in our example above instead of using an auto-generated URI for Amsterdam, one might like to use a DBpedia URL instead.

Conversion tools are often used in two capacities. One is to expose a relational database directly as a SPARQL endpoint. The second is to convert in bulk a database to RDF, which can then be uploaded to a triple store. This later capacity is often done when integrating instance data with ontologies that need to be reasoned over. A good tool to begin with is D2R Server[23] as it provides both capacities in a fairly simple package.

---

[23] http://www4.wiwiss.fu-berlin.de/bizer/d2r-server/.

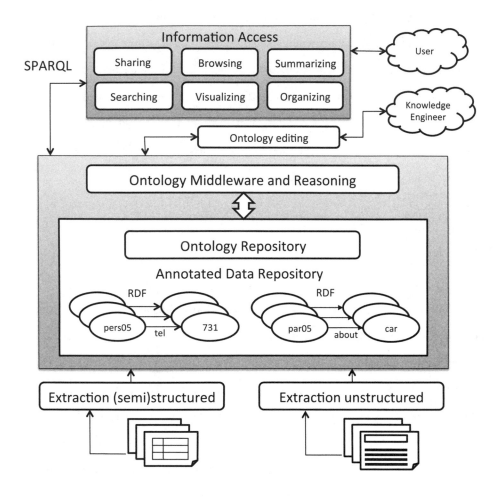

Figure 7.1: Semantic Web knowledge management architecture

7.7   Semantic Web Application Architecture

Building the Semantic Web not only involves using the new languages described in this book but also a rather different style of engineering and a rather different approach to application integration. To illustrate this, we give an overview of how a number of Semantic Web–related tools can be integrated in a single lightweight application architecture using Semantic Web standards to achieve interoperability between independently engineered tools (see figure 7.1).

7.7.1 Knowledge Acquisition

At the bottom of figure 7.1 we find tools that use surface analysis techniques to obtain content from documents. These can be either unstructured natural language documents or structured and semistructured documents (such as databases, HTML tables, and spreadsheets).

In the case of unstructured documents, the tools typically use a combination of statistical techniques and shallow natural language technology to extract key concepts from documents.

In the case of more structured documents, one can use database conversion tools as described above. Induction and pattern recognition techniques can be used to extract the content from more weakly structured documents.

7.7.2 Knowledge Storage

The output of the analysis tools is sets of concepts, organized in a shallow concept hierarchy with at best very few cross-taxonomical relationships, which along with RDF and RDF Schema are sufficiently expressive to represent the extracted information. This information also includes instance data.

Besides simply storing the knowledge produced by the extraction tools, the repository must of course provide the ability to retrieve this knowledge, preferably using a structured query language such as SPARQL. Any reasonable RDF Schema repository will also support the RDF model theory, which includes the deduction of class membership based on domain and range definitions and the derivation of the transitive closure of the subClassOf relationship.

Note that the repository will store both the ontology (class hierarchy, property definitions) and the instances of the ontology (specific individuals that belong to classes, pairs of individuals between which a specific property holds).

7.7.3   Knowledge Maintenance

Besides basic storage and retrieval functionality, a practical Semantic Web repository provides functionality for managing and maintaining the ontology: change management, access and ownership rights, and transaction management.

Besides lightweight ontologies that are automatically generated from unstructured and semistructured data, there must be support for human engineering of much more knowledge-intensive ontologies. Sophisticated editing environments can be used to retrieve ontologies from the repository, allow a knowledge engineer to manipulate them, and place them back in the repository.

7.7.4   Knowledge Use

The ontologies and data in the repository are to be used by applications that serve an end user. We have already described a number of such applications. In addition, external applications may access the knowledge through the exposure of data through one or all of the following approaches: a SPARQL endpoint, Linked Data, or RDFa.

7.7.5   Applying the Architecture

In the On-To-Knowledge project,[24] the architecture of figure 7.1 was implemented with very lightweight connections between the components. Syntactic interoperability was achieved because all components communicated in RDF. Semantic interoperability was achieved because all semantics was expressed using RDF Schema. Physical interoperability was achieved because all communications between components were established using simple HTTP connections, and all but one of the components (the ontology editor) were implemented as remote services. When operating the On-To-Knowledge system from Amsterdam, the ontology extraction tool, running in Norway, was given a London-based URL of a document to analyze; the resulting RDF and RDF Schema

---

[24]http://www.ontoknowledge.org/.

were uploaded to a repository server running in Amersfoort (the Netherlands). These data were uploaded into a locally installed ontology editor, and after editing, downloaded back into the Amersfoort server. The data were then used to drive a Swedish ontology-based website generator as well as a United Kingdom-based search engine, both displaying their results in the browser on the screen in Amsterdam.

In summary, all these tools were running remotely, were independently engineered, and only relied on HTTP and RDF to obtain a high degree of interoperability.

7.7.6 Frameworks

There are a number of frameworks that implement the above architecture. For example, the Drupal content management system[25] adds semantic support to a widely used content management system. There are also two widely used and well-supported open source frameworks: Jena[26] and Sesame.[27] Finally, companies such as Kasabi and Dydra provide hosted frameworks for building Semantic Web applications.

---

[25]http://semantic-drupal.com/.
[26]http://jena.sourceforge.net/.
[27]http://openrdf.org.

Suggested Reading

Some key papers that were used as the basis for this chapter:

- N. Noy and D. McGuinness. Ontology Development 101: A Guide to Creating Your First Ontology.
  www.ksl.stanford.edu/people/dlm/papers/ontology101/
  ontology101-noy-mcguinness.html.

- B. Omelayenko. Learning of Ontologies for the Web: The Analysis of Existing Approaches. In *Proceedings of the International Workshop on Web Dynamics, 8th International Conference on Database Theory (ICDT 2001)*. 2001.
  www.cs.vu.nl/~borys/papers/WebDyn01.pdf.

- Satya S. Sahoo, Wolfgang Halb, Sebastian Hellmann, Kingsley Idehen, Ted Thibodeau Jr, Sören Auer, Juan Sequeda, and Ahmed Ezzat. A Survey of Current Approaches for Mapping of Relational Databases to RDF (PDF). W3CW3C RDB2RDF Incubator Group 2009-01-31.
  http://www.w3.org/2005/Incubator/rdb2rdf/RDB2RDF_SurveyReport.pdf.

- M. Uschold and M. Gruninger. Ontologies: Principles, Methods and Applications. *Knowledge Engineering Review*, Volume 11, 2 (1996): 93–155.

Two often-cited books:

- J. Davies, D. Fensel, and F. van Harmelen. *Towards the Semantic Web: Ontology-Driven Knowledge Management*. New York: Wiley, 2003.

- A. Maedche. *Ontology Learning for the Semantic Web*. New York: Springer 2002.

Exercises and Projects

This project of medium difficulty can be done by two or three people in about two or three weeks. All required software is freely available. We provide some pointers to software that we have used successfully, but given the very active state of development of the field, the availability of software is likely to change rapidly. Also, if certain software is not mentioned, this does not indicate our disapproval of it.

The assignment consists of three parts.

1. In the first part, you will create an ontology that describes the domain and contains the information needed by your own application. You will use the terms defined in the ontology to describe concrete data. In this step you will be applying the methodology for ontology construction outlined in the first part of this chapter and using OWL as a representation language for your ontology (see chapter 4).

2. In the second part, you will use your ontology to construct different views on your data, and you will query the ontology and the data to extract information needed for each view. In this part, you will be applying RDF storage and querying facilities (see chapter 2).

3. In the third part, you will create different graphic presentations of the extracted data using web-based technology.

Part I. Creating an Ontology

As a first step, decide on an application domain, preferably one in which you have sufficient knowledge or for which you have easy access to an expert with that knowledge.

In this description of the project, we use the domain of radio and television broadcasting, with its programs, broadcasting schedules, channels, genres, and celebrities. Of course, you can replace this with any domain of your choosing. In our own courses, we use different domains every year ranging from university ranking to movies and the Fortune 500.

Second, you will build an ontology expressed in OWL that describes the domain (for example, your faculty). The ontology does not have to cover the whole domain but should contain at least a few dozen classes. Pay special attention to the quality (breadth, depth) of the ontology, and aim to use as much of OWL's expressiveness as possible. There are a number of possible tools to use at this stage. Arguably the best current editor is Protégé,[28] but we have also had good experiences with TopBraid Composer.[29]

If you are ambitious, you may even want to start your ontology development by using ontology extraction tools from text or experimenting with tools that allow you to import semistructured data sources, such as Excel sheets or tab-delimited files (see, for example, Excel2RDF, ConvertToRDF, Any23, or XLWrap). Of course, you may choose to start from some existing ontologies in this area.

Preferably, also use an inference engine to validate your ontology and to check it for inconsistencies. If you use Protégé, you may want to exploit some of the available plug-ins for this editor, such as multiple visualizations for your ontology or reasoning with Pellet or HermiT.

Third, populate your ontology with concrete instances and their properties. Depending on the choice of editing tool, this can either be done with the same tool (Protégé) or, given the simple syntactic structure of instances in RDF, you may even decide to write these by hand or to code some simple scripts to extract the instance information from available sources. For example, you can convert a relational database with the given data to RDF. Or you may want to write a scraper for some of the many websites that contain information on radio and television schedules, programs, genres, and celebrities. The BBC even offers a convenient application programming interface for querying their schedule directly.[30] You may want to use the syntax validation service

---

[28] http://protege.stanford.edu/.

[29] See http://topquadrant.com/products/TB_Composer.html.

[30] See http://www.bbc.co.uk/programmes/developers.

offered by W3C[31] – this service not only validates your files for syntactic correctness but also provides a visualization of the existing triples. Also, at this stage, you may be able to experiment with some of the tools that allow you to import data from semistructured sources.

At the end of this step, you should be able to produce the following:

- The full OWL ontology

- Instances of the ontology, described in RDF

- A report describing the scope of the ontology and the main design decisions you made while modeling it.

Part II. Profile Building with SPARQL Queries

Here you will use query facilities to extract relevant parts of your ontology and data. For this you need some way of storing your ontology in a repository that supports both query and reasoning facilities. You may use the Sesame RDF storage and query facility,[32] which comes bundled with an OWLIM reasoner. We have also found that the Joseki Sparql Server is a nice starting point as it provides a built-in web server.

The first step is to upload your ontology (as RDF/XML or Turtle) and associated instances to the repository. This may involve some installation effort.

Next, use the SPARQL query language to define different user profiles, and use queries to extract the data relevant for each profile.

In the example of modeling television programs, you may choose to define viewing guides for people with particular preferences (sports, current affairs) or viewers of particular age groups (e.g., minors), to collect data from multiple television stations (even across nations), to produce presentations for access over broadband or slower mobile connections, and so on.

---

[31]www.w3.org/RDF/Validator/.
[32]www.openrdf.org/.

The output of the queries that define a profile will typically be in XML or JSON (JavaScript Object Notation).

Part III. Presenting Profile-Based Information

Use the output of the queries from part II to generate a human-readable presentation of the different profiles. There exist several convenient libraries for querying a SPARQL endpoint from your favorite programming language: Python has SPARQLWrapper,[33] PHP has the ARC2 library,[34] and Java users will like ARQ, which is part of the popular Jena library.[35] There are even libraries for visualizing SPARQL results from Javascript, such as sgvizler.[36]

The challenge of this part is to define browsable, highly interlinked presentations of the data that were generated and selected in parts I and II.

Alternative Choice of Domain

Besides using the semistructured dataset describing the broadcasting domain, it is possible to model the domain of a university faculty, with its teachers, courses, and departments. In that case, you can use online sources, such as information from the faculty's phonebook, curriculum descriptions, teaching schedules, and so on to scrape both ontology and instance data. Example profiles for this domain could be profiles for students from different years, profiles for students from abroad, profiles for students and teachers, and so on.

Conclusion

After you have finished all parts of this project, you will effectively have implemented large parts of the architecture shown in figure 7.1. You will have used most of the

---

[33] http://sparql-wrapper.sourceforge.net/.
[34] http://incubator.apache.org/jena/documentation/query/index.html.
[35] http://incubator.apache.org/jena/.
[36] code.google.com/p/sgvizler/.

languages described in this book (RDF, RDF Schema, SPARQL, OWL2), and you will have built a genuine Semantic Web application: modeling a part of the world in an ontology, using querying to define user-specific views on this ontology, and using web technology to define browsable presentations of such user-specific views.

Chapter 8

Conclusion

The Semantic Web vision is a reality. As discussed in chapter 6, increasing numbers of companies, governments, and users are adopting the set of standards, technologies, and approaches laid out in this book. We have seen how leveraging the concepts of the web with a flexible data model, RDF, enables the exchange and reuse of information between applications. Based on this data model, we have seen how progressively richer semantics have been added, allowing increasingly powerful inferences to be made (chapter 2). OWL2 (chapter 4) allows for rich knowledge representations to be built and rule languages (chapter 5) allow application-specific inferences to be systematically encoded. All this information is made available through a web-integrated query language SPARQL (chapter 3). Finally, we have seen how ontology engineering methods can be applied to use these technologies in the creation of smarter, more advanced applications (chapter 6).

Throughout this book, we have seen how these technologies and techniques are grounded in knowledge brought from a wide variety of computer science disciplines including Artificial Intelligence, Databases, and Distributed Systems, and pointed to places for further study of all the material given here. The reader is encouraged to study these areas in more depth.

8.1   Principles

The study of the Semantic Web is not only a study in applications or technologies; it also provides a set of general principles that are useful in designing systems even when they do not use Semantic Web approaches. We revisit them again here:

8.1.1   Provide a Path from Lightweight to Heavyweight Technology

Developers and users need simple entry points into technology but also the ability to add more complexity as their needs grow. This notion of a transition path has been successfully applied in the Semantic Web. For example, one can start off with a simple data model in RDF and transition to the richer and more powerful language of OWL. Even in OWL one has a range of choices, from simple rule versions that enable fast inference to the complex descriptions of OWL2 Full.

8.1.2   Standards Save Time

The web and likewise the Semantic Web are facilitated by standards. These standards mean that consumers of information do not have to worry about adapting to every new producer of information. Likewise, producers know that they are giving consumers what they want. There is no need to reinvent syntaxes or models. In the Semantic Web, standards make possible the reuse of information. If I want information about Amsterdam in my application, I no longer have to collect it myself but can build my application on top of all the information available in Wikipedia (in its RDF representation, DBPedia). This ability to reuse saves time in the development and integration of applications. The Semantic Web community is continuing to learn the benefits of standards. Increasingly, there is a move to not only standardize formats and technologies but also ontologies and other content.

8.1.3   Linking Is Vital

The power of the Semantic Web, like the web, is in its links. Links enable knowledge to be distributed across organizations, people, and systems. It enables those who care about knowledge the most to tend to it while still enabling others to access it and find it. Links are lightweight enough to be easily created, while still strong enough to allow for the integration of knowledge. We see this in the Linked Data Cloud where hundreds of specialized datasets can rely on other specialized datasets to provide (in a simple way) more and detailed knowledge about a topic or concept. It seems reasonable to say that in any large information system, the ability to link can predict its success or failure.

8.1.4   A Little Semantics Goes a Long Way

One of the visionaries of the Semantic Web, Jim Hendler, coined the term "A little semantics goes a long way." This phrase emphasizes the importance of the ability to automatically understand the meaning of terms. Sharing data is not enough – one needs to share meaning. Simply knowing that a bank refers to a chair and not a financial institution goes a tremendous way in enabling sophisticated systems. Throughout this book, we have described techniques for adding semantics to data and making use of that in applications. Whether one adopts these particular technologies in a system is one thing, but a key principle to recognize is that semantics can be a differentiating ingredient.

The principles above have helped make the Semantic Web a success but more importantly they are applicable in the design of any large-scale software system or set of technologies.

8.2   Where Next?

The Semantic Web is still growing and changing. Existing technologies are being refined and new ones are being developed. Broadly speaking, there seem to be several major research directions that are actively being studied:

- Reasoning in context. This is the ability to make inferences depending not only on the knowledge given but also on the situation the application is in or where the knowledge came from (its provenance). For example, you may trust a given data source about apartments if you are just at the beginning of your apartment hunt, but not when it comes down to making a final decision.

- Large-scale reasoning. As the amount of data on the Semantic Web has grown, the ability to reason with it has become more difficult. Projects like the Large Knowledge Collidor (http://www.larkc.eu) have shown the ability to do simple rule-style reasoning with billions of triples. However, as the complexity of the semantics grows and the amount of data and knowledge continues to explode, there will be a need for better and faster reasoners.

- Distributed querying. Standard practice today for using distributed sources of knowledge on the Semantic Web is to centralize the knowledge by capturing it from its various sources. This is done for purposes of efficiency. However, it still an open question as to how to use, and in particular query, these distributed sources of information without the need for centralization.

- Streaming knowledge. Semantic Web technologies primarily deal with static or slowly changing information. This situation is rapidly changing as information is being produced by sensors, microblogging, and other sources at an ever-increasing pace. There are open questions about how to extract, reason, and make use of semantics from such streaming data sources.

These are just some of the current research directions being pursued with respect to the Semantic Web. The field itself and its technologies are rapidly changing. While this book provides a core basis, the conclusion to the Semantic Web is far from being written. To read the current story, please see the online supplement: http://www.semanticwebprimer.org.

Appendix A

XML Basics

A.1 The XML Language

An *XML document* consists of a prolog, a number of elements, and an optional epilog (not discussed here).

A.1.1 Prolog

The prolog consists of an XML declaration and an optional reference to external structuring documents. Here is an example of an *XML declaration*:

```
<?xml version="1.0" encoding="UTF-16"?>
```

It specifies that the current document is an XML document, and defines the version and the character encoding used in the particular system (such as UTF-8, UTF-16, and ISO 8859-1). The character encoding is not mandatory, but its specification is considered good practice. Sometimes we also specify whether the document is self-contained – that is, whether it does not refer to external structuring documents:

```
<?xml version="1.0" encoding="UTF-16" standalone="no"?>
```

A reference to external structuring documents looks like this:

```
<!DOCTYPE book SYSTEM "book.dtd">
```

Here the structuring information is found in a local file called book.dtd. Instead, the reference might be a URL. If only a locally recognized name or only a URL is used, then the label SYSTEM is used. If, however, one wishes to give both a local name and a URL, then the label PUBLIC should be used instead.

A.1.2 Elements

XML elements represent the "things" the XML document talks about, such as books, authors, and publishers. They compose the main concept of XML documents. An element consists of an *opening tag*, its *content*, and a *closing tag*. For example,

```
<lecturer>David Billington</lecturer>
```

Tag names can be chosen almost freely; there are very few restrictions. The most important restrictions are that the first character must be a letter, an underscore, or a colon, and that no name may begin with the string "xml" in any combination of cases (such as "Xml" and "xML").

The content may be text, other elements, or nothing. For example,

```
<lecturer>
  <name>David Billington</name>
  <phone>+61-7-3875 507</phone>
</lecturer>
```

If there is no content, then the element is called *empty*. An empty element like

```
<lecturer></lecturer>
```

can be abbreviated as

```
<lecturer/>
```

A.1.3   Attributes

An empty element is not necessarily meaningless, because it may have some properties
in terms of *attributes*. An attribute is a name-value pair inside the opening tag of an
element:

```
<lecturer name="David Billington" phone="+61-7-3875 507"/>
```

Here is an example of attributes for a nonempty element:

```
<order orderNo="23456" customer="John Smith"
        date="October 15, 2002">
  <item itemNo="a528" quantity="1"/>
  <item itemNo="c817" quantity="3"/>
</order>
```

The same information could have been written as follows, replacing attributes with
nested elements:

```
<order>
  <orderNo>23456</orderNo>
  <customer>John Smith</customer>
  <date>October 15, 2002</date>
  <item>
    <itemNo>a528</itemNo>
    <quantity>1</quantity>
  </item>
  <item>
    <itemNo>c817</itemNo>
    <quantity>3</quantity>
  </item>
</order>
```

When to use elements and when attributes is often a matter of taste. However, note that attributes cannot be nested.

A.1.4   Comments

A comment is a piece of text that is to be ignored by the parser. It has the form

```
<!-- This is a comment -->
```

A.1.5   Processing Instructions (PIs)

PIs provide a mechanism for passing information to an application about how to handle elements. The general form is

```
<?target instruction?>
```

For example,

```
<?stylesheet type="text/css" href="mystyle.css"?>
```

PIs offer procedural possibilities in an otherwise declarative environment.

A.1.6   Well-Formed XML Documents

An XML document is well-formed if it is syntactically correct. The following are some syntactic rules:

- There is only one outermost element in the document (called the *root element*).

- Each element contains an opening and a corresponding closing tag.

- Tags may not overlap, as in

  ```
  <author><name>Lee Hong</author></name>.
  ```

- Attributes within an element have unique names.

- Element and tag names must be permissible.

A.1.7   Tree Model of XML Documents

It is possible to represent well-formed XML documents as trees; thus trees provide a formal data model for XML. This representation is often instructive. As an example, consider the following document:

```
<?xml version="1.0" encoding="UTF-16"?>
<!DOCTYPE email SYSTEM "email.dtd">
<email>
  <head>
    <from   name="Michael Maher"
            address="michaelmaher@cs.gu.edu.au"/>
    <to      name="Grigoris Antoniou"
            address="grigoris@cs.unibremen.de"/>
    <subject>Where is your draft?</subject>
  </head>
  <body>
  Grigoris, where is the draft of the paper
  you promised me last week?
  </body>
</email>
```

Figure A.1 shows the tree representation of this XML document. It is an ordered, labeled tree:

- There is exactly one root.

- There are no cycles.

- Each node, other than the root, has exactly one parent.

- Each node has a label.

- The order of elements is important.

However, while the order of elements is important, the order of attributes is not. So, the following two elements are equivalent:

```
<person lastname="Woo" firstname="Jason"/>
<person firstname="Jason" lastname="Woo"/>
```

This aspect is not represented properly in the tree. In general, we would require a more refined tree concept; for example, we should also differentiate between the different types of nodes (element node, attribute node, etc.). However, here we use graphs as illustrations, so we do not go into further detail.

Figure A.1 also shows the difference between the *root* (representing the XML document), and the *root element*, in our case the email element. This distinction will play a role when we discuss addressing and querying XML documents.

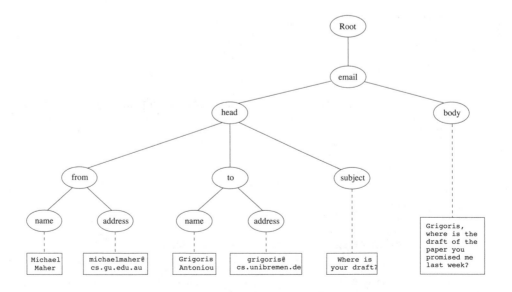

Figure A.1: Tree representation of an XML document

A.2 Structuring

An XML document is well-formed if it respects certain syntactic rules. However, those rules say nothing specific about the structure of the document. Now, imagine two applications that try to communicate, and that wish to use the same vocabulary. For this purpose it is necessary to define all the element and attribute names that may be used. Moreover, the structure should also be defined: what values an attribute may take, which elements may or must occur within other elements, and so on.

In the presence of such structuring information we have an enhanced possibility of document validation. We say that an XML document is *valid* if it is well-formed, uses structuring information, and respects that structuring information.

There are two ways of defining the structure of XML documents: DTDs, the older and more restricted way, and XML Schema, which offers extended possibilities, mainly for the definition of data types.

A.2.1 DTDs

External and Internal DTDs

The components of a DTD can be defined in a separate file (*external DTD*) or within the XML document itself (*internal DTD*). Usually it is better to use external DTDs, because their definitions can be used across several documents; otherwise duplication is inevitable, and the maintenance of consistency over time becomes difficult.

Elements

Consider the element

```
<lecturer>
 <name>David Billington</name>
 <phone>+61-7-3875 507</phone>
</lecturer>
```

from the previous section. A DTD for this element type[1] looks like this:

```
<!ELEMENT lecturer (name,phone)>
<!ELEMENT name (#PCDATA)>
<!ELEMENT phone (#PCDATA)>
```

The meaning of this DTD is as follows:

- The element types lecturer, name, and phone may be used in the document.

- A lecturer element contains a name element and a phone element, in that order.

- A name element and a phone element may have any content. In DTDs, #PCDATA is the only atomic type for elements.

We express that a lecturer element contains either a name element or a phone element as follows:

```
<!ELEMENT lecturer (name|phone)>
```

It gets more difficult when we wish to specify that a lecturer element contains a name element and a phone element *in any order*. We can only use the trick

```
<!ELEMENT lecturer ((name,phone)|(phone,name))>
```

However, this approach suffers from practical limitations (imagine ten elements in any order).

Attributes

Consider the element

---

[1]The distinction between the element type lecturer and a particular element of this type, such as David Billington, should be clear. All particular elements of type lecturer (referred to as lecturer elements) share the same structure, which is defined here.

```
<order orderNo="23456" customer="John Smith"
          date="October 15, 2002">
   <item itemNo="a528" quantity="1"/>
   <item itemNo="c817" quantity="3"/>
</order>
```

from the previous section. A DTD for it looks like this:

```
<!ELEMENT order (item+)>
<!ATTLIST order
     orderNo      ID      #REQUIRED
     customer   CDATA #REQUIRED
     date         CDATA #REQUIRED>
<!ELEMENT item EMPTY>
<!ATTLIST item
     itemNo      ID      #REQUIRED
     quantity    CDATA #REQUIRED
     comments  CDATA #IMPLIED>
```

Compared to the previous example, a new aspect is that the item element type is defined to be empty. Another new aspect is the appearance of + after item in the definition of the order element type. It is one of the *cardinality operators*:

?: appears zero times or once.

*: appears zero or more times.

+: appears one or more times.

No cardinality operator means exactly once.

In addition to defining elements, we have to define attributes. This is done in an *attribute list*. The first component is the name of the element type to which the list applies, followed by a list of triplets of attribute name, attribute type, and value type. An *attribute* name is a name that may be used in an XML document using a DTD.

Attribute Types

Attribute types are similar to predefined data types, but the selection is very limited. The most important attribute types are

- CDATA, a string (sequence of characters),

- ID, a name that is unique across the entire XML document,

- IDREF, a reference to another element with an ID attribute carrying the same value as the IDREF attribute,

- IDREFS, a series of IDREFs,

- $(v_1 | \ldots | v_n)$, an enumeration of all possible values.

The selection is not satisfactory. For example, dates and numbers cannot be specified; they have to be interpreted as strings (CDATA); thus their specific structure cannot be enforced.

Value Types

There are four value types:

- #REQUIRED. The attribute must appear in every occurrence of the element type in the XML document. In the previous example, itemNo and quantity must always appear within an item element.

- #IMPLIED. The appearance of the attribute is optional. In the example, comments are optional.

- #FIXED "value". Every element must have this attribute, which always has the value given after #FIXED in the DTD. A value given in an XML document is meaningless because it is overridden by the fixed value.

- "value". This specifies the default value for the attribute. If a specific value appears in the XML document, it overrides the default value. For example, the default encoding of the email system may be "mime", but "binhex" will be used if specified explicitly by the user.

Referencing

Here is an example for the use of IDREF and IDREFS. First we give a DTD:

```
<!ELEMENT family (person*)>
<!ELEMENT person (name)>
<!ELEMENT name (#PCDATA)>
<!ATTLIST person
    id        ID      #REQUIRED
    mother    IDREF   #IMPLIED
    father    IDREF   #IMPLIED
    children  IDREFS  #IMPLIED>
```

An XML element that respects this DTD is the following:

```
<family>

    <person id="bob" mother="mary" father="peter">
      <name>Bob Marley</name>
    </person>

    <person id="bridget" mother="mary">
      <name>Bridget Jones</name>
```

```
</person>

<person id="mary" children="bob bridget">
  <name>Mary Poppins</name>
</person>

<person id="peter" children="bob">
  <name>Peter Marley</name>
</person>

</family>
```

Readers should study the references between persons.

XML Entities

An XML entity can play several roles, such as a placeholder for repeatable characters (a type of shorthand), a section of external data (e.g., XML or other), or as a part of a declaration for elements. For example, suppose that a document has several copyright notices that refer to the current year. Then it makes sense to declare an entity

```
<!ENTITY thisyear "2007">
```

Then, at each place the current year needs to be included, we can use the entity reference &thisyear; instead. That way, updating the year value to "2008" for the whole document will only mean changing the entity declaration.

A Concluding Example

As a final example we give a DTD for the email element presented previously:

```
<!ELEMENT email (head,body)>
<!ELEMENT head (from,to+,cc*,subject)>
```

```
<!ELEMENT from EMPTY>
<!ATTLIST from
    name      CDATA      #IMPLIED
    address   CDATA      #REQUIRED>
<!ELEMENT to EMPTY>
<!ATTLIST to
    name      CDATA      #IMPLIED
    address   CDATA      #REQUIRED>
<!ELEMENT cc EMPTY>
<!ATTLIST cc
    name      CDATA      #IMPLIED
    address   CDATA      #REQUIRED>
<!ELEMENT subject (#PCDATA)>
<!ELEMENT body (text,attachment*)>
<!ELEMENT text (#PCDATA)>
<!ELEMENT attachment EMPTY>
<!ATTLIST attachment
    encoding   (mime|binhex) "mime"
    file       CDATA      #REQUIRED>
```

We go through some interesting parts of this DTD:

- A head element contains a from element, at least one to element, zero or more cc elements, and a subject element, in that order.

- In from, to, and cc elements the name attribute is not required; the address attribute, on the other hand, is always required.

- A body element contains a text element, possibly followed by a number of attachment elements.

- The encoding attribute of an attachment element must have either the value "mime" or "binhex", the former being the default value.

We conclude with two more remarks on DTDs. First, a DTD can be interpreted as an Extended Backus-Naur Form (EBNF). For example, the declaration

```
<!ELEMENT email (head,body)>
```

is equivalent to the rule

```
email ::= head body
```

which means that an email consists of a head followed by a body. And second, recursive definitions are possible in DTDs. For example,

```
<!ELEMENT bintree ((bintree root bintree)|emptytree)>
```

defines binary trees: a binary tree is the empty tree, or consists of a left subtree, a root, and a right subtree.

A.2.2   XML Schema

XML Schema offers a significantly richer language for defining the structure of XML documents. One of its characteristics is that its syntax is based on XML itself. This design decision provides a significant improvement in readability, but more important, it also allows significant reuse of technology. It is no longer necessary to write separate parsers, editors, pretty printers, and so on to obtain a separate syntax, as was required for DTDs; any XML will do. An even more important improvement is the possibility of reusing and refining schemas. XML Schema allows one to define new types by extending or restricting already existing ones. In combination with an XML-based syntax, this feature allows one to build schemas from other schemas, thus reducing the workload. Finally, XML Schema provides a sophisticated set of data types that can be used in XML documents (DTDs were limited to strings only).

An XML schema is an element with an opening tag like

```
<xsd:schema
   xmlns:xsd="http://www.w3.org/2000/10/XMLSchema"
   version="1.0">
```

The element uses the schema of XML Schema found at the W3C website. It is, so to speak, the foundation on which new schemas can be built. The prefix xsd denotes the namespace of that schema (more on namespaces in the next section). If the prefix is omitted in the xmlns attribute, then we are using elements from this namespace by default:

```
<schema
   xmlns="http://www.w3.org/2000/10/XMLSchema"
   version="1.0">
```

In the following we omit the xsd prefix.

Now we turn to schema elements. Their most important contents are the definitions of element and attribute types, which are defined using data types.

Element Types

The syntax of element types is

```
<element name="..."/>
```

and they may have a number of optional attributes, such as types,

```
type="..."
```

or cardinality constraints

- minOccurs="x", where x may be any natural number (including zero),

- maxOccurs="x", where x may be any natural number (including zero) or unbounded.

minOccurs and maxOccurs are generalizations of the cardinality operators ?, *, and +, offered by DTDs. When cardinality constraints are not provided explicitly, minOccurs and maxOccurs have value 1 by default.

Here are a few examples.

```
<element name="email"/>
```

```
<element name="head" minOccurs="1" maxOccurs="1"/>
```

```
<element name="to" minOccurs="1"/>
```

Attribute Types

The syntax of attribute types is

```
<attribute name="..."/>
```

and they may have a number of optional attributes, such as types,

```
type="..."
```

or existence (corresponds to #OPTIONAL and #IMPLIED in DTDs),

```
use="x", where x may be optional or required or prohibited,
```

or a default value (corresponds to #FIXED and default values in DTDs).

Here are examples:

```
<attribute name="id" type="ID" use="required"/>
```

```
<attribute name="speaks" type="Language" use="optional"
    default="en"/>
```

Data Types

We have already recognized the very restricted selection of data types as a key weakness of DTDs. XML Schema provides powerful capabilities for defining data type. First there is a variety of *built-in data types*. Here we list a few:

- Numerical data types, including integer, short, Byte, long, float, decimal

- String data types, including string, ID, IDREF, CDATA, language

- Date and time data types, including time, date, gMonth, gYear

There are also *user-defined data types*, comprising *simple data types*, which cannot use elements or attributes, and *complex data types*, which can use elements and attributes. We discuss complex types first, deferring discussion of simple data types until we talk about restriction. Complex types are defined from already existing data types by defining some attributes (if any) and using

- sequence, a sequence of existing data type elements, the appearance of which in a predefined order is important,

- all, a collection of elements that must appear but the order of which is not important,

- choice, a collection of elements, of which one will be chosen.

Here is an example:

```
<complexType name="lecturerType">
  <sequence>
    <element name="firstname" type="string"
      minOccurs="0" maxOccurs="unbounded"/>
    <element name="lastname" type="string"/>
  </sequence>
```

```
        <attribute name="title" type="string" use="optional"/>
    </complexType>
```

The meaning is that an element in an XML document that is declared to be of type lecturerType may have a title attribute; it may also include any number of firstname elements and must include exactly one lastname element.

Data Type Extension

Already existing data types can be extended by new elements or attributes. As an example, we extend the lecturer data type.

```
    <complexType name="extendedLecturerType">
      <complexContent>
        <extension base="lecturerType">
          <sequence>
            <element name="email" type="string"
                minOccurs="0" maxOccurs="1"/>
          </sequence>
          <attribute name="rank" type="string" use="required"/>
        </extension>
      </complexContent>
    </complexType>
```

In this example, lecturerType is extended by an email element and a rank attribute. The resulting data type looks like this:

```
    <complexType name="extendedLecturerType">
      <sequence>
        <element name="firstname" type="string"
          minOccurs="0" maxOccurs="unbounded"/>
        <element name="lastname" type="string"/>
```

```
      <element name="email" type="string"
        minOccurs="0" maxOccurs="1"/>
    </sequence>
    <attribute name="title" type="string" use="optional"/>
    <attribute name="rank" type="string" use="required"/>
  </complexType>
```

A hierarchical relationship exists between the original and the extended type. *Instances of the extended type are also instances of the original type.* They may contain additional information, but neither less information nor information of the wrong type.

Data Type Restriction

An existing data type may also be restricted by adding constraints on certain values. For example, new type and use attributes may be added, or the numerical constraints of minOccurs and maxOccurs tightened.

It is important to understand that restriction is *not* the opposite process of extension. Restriction is not achieved by deleting elements or attributes. Therefore, the following hierarchical relationship still holds: *Instances of the restricted type are also instances of the original type.* They satisfy at least the constraints of the original type and some new ones.

As an example, we restrict the lecturer data type as follows:

```
<complexType name="restrictedLecturerType">
  <complexContent>
    <restriction base="lecturerType">
      <sequence>
        <element name="firstname" type="string"
          minOccurs="1" maxOccurs="2"/>
      </sequence>
      <attribute name="title" type="string" use="required"/>
```

```
  </restriction>
 </complexContent>
</complexType>
```

The tightened constraints are shown in boldface. Readers should compare them with the original ones.

Simple data types can also be defined by restricting existing data types. For example, we can define a type dayOfMonth that admits values from 1 to 31 as follows:

```
<simpleType name="dayOfMonth">
  <restriction base="integer">
    <minInclusive value="1"/>
    <maxInclusive value="31"/>
  </restriction>
</simpleType>
```

It is also possible to define a data type by listing all the possible values. For example, we can define a data type dayOfWeek as follows:

```
<simpleType name="dayOfWeek">
  <restriction base="string">
    <enumeration value="Mon"/>
    <enumeration value="Tue"/>
    <enumeration value="Wed"/>
    <enumeration value="Thu"/>
    <enumeration value="Fri"/>
    <enumeration value="Sat"/>
    <enumeration value="Sun"/>
  </restriction>
</simpleType>
```

A Concluding Example

Here we define an XML schema for email, so that it can be compared to the DTD provided earlier.

```
<element name="email" type="emailType"/>
<complexType name="emailType">
  <sequence>
    <element name="head" type="headType"/>
    <element name="body" type="bodyType"/>
  </sequence>
</complexType>


<complexType name="headType">
  <sequence>
    <element name="from" type="nameAddress"/>
    <element name="to" type="nameAddress"
      minOccurs="1" maxOccurs="unbounded"/>
    <element name="cc" type="nameAddress"
      minOccurs="0" maxOccurs="unbounded"/>
    <element name="subject" type="string"/>
  </sequence>
</complexType>


<complexType name="nameAddress">
  <attribute name="name" type="string" use="optional"/>
  <attribute name="address" type="string" use="required"/>
</complexType>


<complexType name="bodyType">
  <sequence>
```

```
<element name="text" type="string"/>
<element name="attachment" minOccurs="0"
    maxOccurs="unbounded">
  <complexType>
    <attribute name="encoding" use="optional"
        default="mime">
      <simpleType>
        <restriction base="string">
          <enumeration value="mime"/>
          <enumeration value="binhex"/>
        </restriction>
      </simpleType>
    </attribute>
    <attribute name="file" type="string"
        use="required"/>
  </complexType>
</element>
</sequence>
</complexType>
```

Note that some data types are defined separately and given names, while others are defined within other types and defined anonymously (the types for the attachment element and the encoding attribute). In general, if a type is used only once, it makes sense to define it anonymously for local use. However, this approach reaches its limitations quickly if nesting becomes too deep.

A.3 Namespaces

One of the main advantages of using XML as a universal (meta) markup language is that information from various sources may be accessed; in technical terms, an XML document may use more than one DTD or schema. But since each structuring document is developed independently, *name clashes* appear inevitable. If DTD A and DTD B define an element type e in different ways, a parser trying to validate an XML document in which an e element appears must be told which DTD to use for validation purposes.

The technical solution is simple: disambiguation is achieved by using a different prefix for each DTD or schema. The prefix is separated from the local name by a colon:

```
prefix:name
```

As an example, consider an (imaginary) joint venture of an Australian university, say, Griffith University, and an American university, say, the University of Kentucky, to present a unified view for online students. Each university uses its own terminology, and there are differences. For example, lecturers in the United States are not considered regular faculty, whereas in Australia they are (in fact, they correspond to assistant professors in the United States). The following example shows how disambiguation can be achieved.

```
<?xml version="1.0" encoding="UTF-16"?>
<vu:instructors
     xmlns:vu="http://www.vu.com/empDTD"
     xmlns:gu="http://www.gu.au/empDTD"
     xmlns:uky="http://www.uky.edu/empDTD">
  <uky:faculty
     uky:title="assistant professor"
     uky:name="John Smith"
     uky:department="Computer Science"/>
  <gu:academicStaff
     gu:title="lecturer"
     gu:name="Mate Jones"
     gu:school="Information Technology"/>
```

```
</vu:instructors>
```

So, namespaces are declared within an element and can be used in that element and any of its children (elements and attributes). A namespace declaration has the form:

```
xmlns:prefix="location"
```

where location may be the address of the DTD or schema. If a prefix is not specified, as in

```
xmlns="location"
```

then the location is used by default. For example, the previous example is equivalent to the following document:

```
<?xml version="1.0" encoding="UTF-16"?>
<vu:instructors
     xmlns:vu="http://www.vu.com/empDTD"
     xmlns="http://www.gu.au/empDTD"
     xmlns:uky="http://www.uky.edu/empDTD">
   <uky:faculty
     uky:title="assistant professor"
     uky:name="John Smith"
     uky:department="Computer Science"/>
   <academicStaff
     title="lecturer"
     name="Mate Jones"
     school="Information Technology"/>
</vu:instructors>
```

A.4 Addressing and Querying XML Documents

In relational databases, parts of a database can be selected and retrieved using query languages such as SQL. The same is true for XML documents, for which there exist a number of proposals for query languages, such as XQL, XML-QL, and XQuery.

The central concept of XML query languages is a *path expression* that specifies how a node, or a set of nodes, in the tree representation of the XML document can be reached. We introduce path expressions in the form of XPath because they can be used for purposes other than querying– namely, for transforming XML documents.

XPath is a language for addressing parts of an XML document. It operates on the tree data model of XML and has a non-XML syntax. The key concepts are path expressions. They can be

- absolute (starting at the root of the tree); syntactically they begin with the symbol /, which refers to the root of the document, situated one level above the root element of the document; or

- relative to a context node.

Consider the following XML document:

```xml
<?xml version="1.0" encoding="UTF-16"?>
<!DOCTYPE library PUBLIC "library.dtd">
<library location="Bremen">
  <author name="Henry Wise">
    <book title="Artificial Intelligence"/>
    <book title="Modern Web Services"/>
    <book title="Theory of Computation"/>
  </author>
  <author name="William Smart">
    <book title="Artificial Intelligence"/>
```

```
    </author>
    <author name="Cynthia Singleton">
        <book title="The Semantic Web"/>
        <book title="Browser Technology Revised"/>
    </author>
</library>
```

Its tree representation is shown in figure A.2.

In the following we illustrate the capabilities of XPath with a few examples of path expressions.

1. Address all author elements.

   /library/author

   This path expression addresses all author elements that are children of the library element node, which resides immediately below the root. Using a sequence $/t_1/\ldots/t_n$, where each t_{i+1} is a child node of t_i, we define a path through the tree representation.

2. An alternative solution for the previous example is

   //author

   Here // says that we should consider all elements in the document and check whether they are of type author. In other words, this path expression addresses all author elements anywhere in the document. Because of the specific structure of our XML document, this expression and the previous one lead to the same result; however, they may lead to different results, in general.

3. Address the location attribute nodes within library element nodes.

   /library/@location

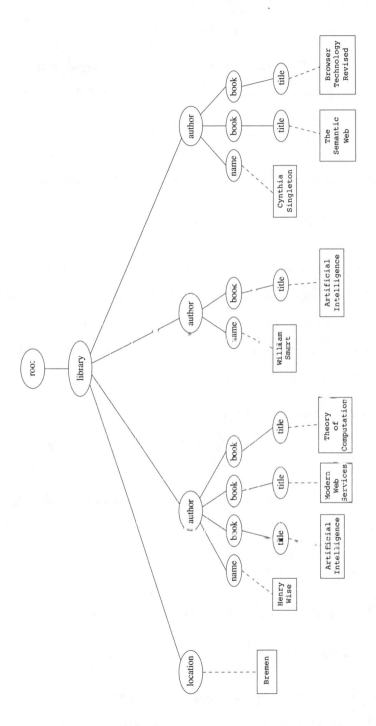

Figure A.2: Tree representation of a library document

The symbol @ is used to denote attribute nodes.

4. Address all title attribute nodes within book elements anywhere in the document that have the value "Artificial Intelligence" (see figure A.3).

    ```
    //book/@title=[.="Artificial Intelligence"]
    ```

5. Address all books with title "Artificial Intelligence" (see figure A.4).

    ```
    //book[@title="Artificial Intelligence"]
    ```

We call a test within square brackets a *filter expression*. It restricts the set of addressed nodes. Note the difference between this expression and the one in query 4. Here we address book elements the title of which satisfies a certain condition. In query 4 we collected title attribute nodes of book elements. A comparison of figures A.3 and A.4 illustrates the difference.

6. Address the first author element node in the XML document.

    ```
    //author[1]
    ```

7. Address the last book element within the first author element node in the document.

    ```
    //author[1]/book[last()]
    ```

8. Address all book element nodes without a title attribute.

    ```
    //book[not (@title)]
    ```

These examples are meant to give a feeling of the expressive power of path expressions. In general, a path expression consists of a series of steps separated by slashes. A *step* consists of an axis specifier, a node test, and an optional predicate.

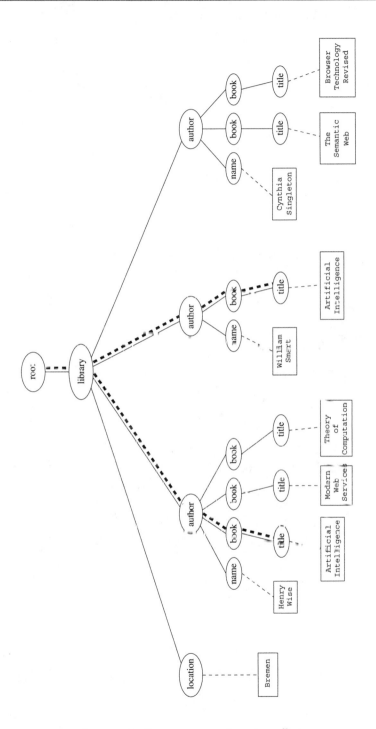

Figure A.3: Tree representation of query 4

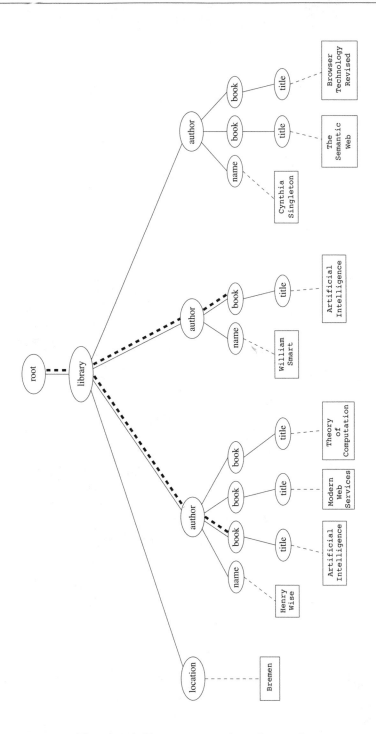

Figure A.4: Tree representation of query 5

- An *axis specifier* determines the tree relationship between the nodes to be addressed and the context node. Examples are parent, ancestor, child (the default), sibling, and attribute node. // is such an axis specifier; it denotes descendant or self.

- A *node test* specifies which nodes to address. The most common node tests are element names (which may use namespace information), but there are others. For example, * addresses all element nodes, comment() all comment nodes, and so on.

- *Predicates* (or *filter expressions*) are optional and are used to refine the set of addressed nodes. For example, the expression [1] selects the first node, [position()=last()] selects the last node, [position() mod 2 = 0] the even nodes, and so on.

We have only presented the abbreviated syntax, but XPath actually has a more complicated full syntax. References are found at the end of this appendix.

A.5   Processing

So far we have not provided any information about how XML documents can be displayed. Such information is necessary because unlike HTML documents, XML documents do not contain formatting information. The advantage is that a given XML document can be presented in various ways when different *style sheets* are applied to it. For example, consider the XML element

```
<author>
    <name>Grigoris Antoniou</name>
    <affiliation>University of Bremen</affiliation>
    <email>ga@tzi.de</email>
</author>
```

The output might look like the following, if a style sheet is used:

Grigoris Antoniou

University of Bremen

ga@tzi.de

Or it might appear as follows, if a different style sheet is used:

Grigoris Antoniou

University of Bremen

ga@tzi.de

Style sheets can be written in various languages, such as CSS2 (cascading style sheets level 2). The other possibility is XSL (extensible stylesheet language).

XSL includes both a transformation language (XSLT) and a formatting language. Each of these is, of course, an XML application. XSLT specifies rules with which an input XML document is transformed to another XML document, an HTML document, or plain text. The output document may use the same DTD or schema as the input document, or it may use a completely different vocabulary.

XSLT (XSL transformations) can be used independently of the formatting language. Its ability to move data and metadata from one XML representation to another makes it a most valuable tool for XML-based applications. Generally XSLT is chosen when applications that use different DTDs or schemas need to communicate. XSLT is a tool that can be used for machine-processing of content without any regard to displaying the information for people to read. Despite this fact, in the following we use XSLT only to display XML documents.

One way of defining the presentation of an XML document is to transform it into an HTML document. Here is an example. We define an XSLT document that will be applied to the author example.

```
<?xml version="1.0" encoding="UTF-16"?>
<xsl:stylesheet version="1.0"
      xmlns:xsl="http://www.w3.org/1999/XSL/Transform">


   <xsl:template match="/author">
     <html>
        <head><title>An author< /title></head>
        <body bgcolor="white">
          <b><xsl:value-of select="name"/></b><br></br>
          <xsl:value-of select="affiliation"/><br></br>
          <i><xsl:value-of select="email"/></i>
        </body>
     </html>
   </xsl:template>
</xsl:stylesheet>
```

The output of this style sheet, applied to the previous XML document, produces the following HTML document (which now defines the presentation):

```
<html>
   <head><title>An author< /title></head>
   <body bgcolor="white">
     <b>Grigoris Antoniou</b><br>
     University of Bremen<br>
     <i>ga@tzi.de</i>
   </body>
</html>
```

Let us make a few observations. XSLT documents are XML documents. So XSLT resides on top of XML (that is, it is an XML application). The XSLT document defines a *template*; in this case an HTML document, with some placeholders for content to be

```
<html>
<head><title>An author</title></head>
<body bgcolor="white">
  <b>...</b><br>
  ...<br>
  <i>...</i>
</body>
</html>
```

Figure A.5: A template

inserted (see figure A.5).

In the previous XSLT document, xsl:value-of retrieves the value of an element and copies it into the output document. That is, it places some content into the template.

Now suppose we had an XML document with details of several authors. It would clearly be a waste of effort to treat each author element separately. In such cases, a special template is defined for author elements, and is used by the main template. We illustrate this approach in the following input document:

```
<authors>
  <author>
    <name>Grigoris Antoniou</name>
    <affiliation>University of Bremen</affiliation>
    <email>ga@tzi.de</email>
  </author>
  <author>
    <name>David Billington</name>
    <affiliation>Griffith University</affiliation>
    <email>david@gu.edu.net</email>
  </author>
</authors>
```

We define the following XSLT document:

```
<?xml version="1.0" encoding="UTF-16"?>
<xsl:stylesheet version="1.0"
    xmlns:xsl="http://www.w3.org/1999/XSL/Transform">


  <xsl:template match="/">
    <html>
    <head><title>Authors< /title></head>
    <body bgcolor="white">
       <xsl:apply-templates select="authors"/>
       <!-- Apply templates for AUTHORS children -->
    </body>
    </html>
  </xsl:template>


  <xsl:template match="authors">
     <xsl:apply-templates select="author"/>
  </xsl:template>


  <xsl:template match="author">
     <h2><xsl:value-of select="name"/></h2>
     Affiliation:<xsl:value-of select="affiliation"/><br>
     Email:  <xsl:value-of select="email"/>
     <p>
  </xsl:template>
</xsl:stylesheet>
```

The output produced is

```
<html>
<head><title>Authors< /title></head>
```

```
<body bgcolor="white">

  <h2>Grigoris Antoniou</h2>

  Affiliation: University of Bremen<br>

  Email: ga@tzi.de

  <p>

  <h2>David Billington</h2>

  Affiliation: Griffith University<br>

  Email: david@gu.edu.net

  <p>

</body>

</html>
```

The xsl:apply-templates element causes all children of the context node to be matched against the selected path expression. For example, if the current template applies to / (that is, if the current context node is the root), then the element xsl:apply-templates applies to the root element, which in this case is the authors element (remember that / is located above the root element). And if the current node is the authors element, then the element xsl:apply-templates select="author" causes the template for the author elements to be applied to all author children of the authors element.

It is good practice to define a template for each element type in the document. Even if no specific processing is applied to certain elements, like in our example, the xsl:apply-templates element should be used. That way, we work our way from the root to the leaves of the tree, and all templates are indeed applied.

Now we turn our attention to attributes. Suppose we wish to process the element

```
<person firstname="John" lastname="Woo"/>
```

with XSLT. Let us attempt the easiest task imaginable, a transformation of the element to itself. One might be tempted to write

```
<xsl:template match="person">
```

```
<person
    firstname="<xsl:value-of select="@firstname">"
    lastname="<xsl:value-of select="@lastname">"/>
</xsl:template>
```

However, this is not a well-formed XML document because tags are not allowed within the values of attributes. But the intention is clear; we wish to add attribute values into the template. In XSLT, data enclosed in curly brackets take the place of the xsl:value-of element. The correct way to define a template for this example is as follows:

```
<xsl:template match="person">
    <person
      firstname="{@firstname}"
      lastname="{@lastname}"/>
</xsl:template>
```

Finally, we give a transformation example from one XML document to another, which does not specify the display. Again we use the authors document as input and define an XSLT document as follows:

```
<?xml version="1.0" encoding="UTF-16"?>
<xsl:stylesheet version="1.0"
       xmlns:xsl="http://www.w3.org/1999/XSL/Transform">

    <xsl:template match="/">
      <authors>
        <xsl:apply-templates select="authors"/>
      </authors>
    </xsl:template>
```

```
<xsl:template match="authors">

  <xsl:apply-templates select="author"/>

</xsl:template>


<xsl:template match="author">

  <author>

    <name><xsl:value-of select="name"/></name>

    <contact>

      <institute>

        <xsl:value-of select="affiliation"/>

      </institute>

      <email><xsl:value-of select="email"/></email>

    </contact>

  </author>

</xsl:template>


</xsl:stylesheet>
```

The tree representation of the output document is shown in figure A.6 to illustrate the

tree transformation character of XSLT.

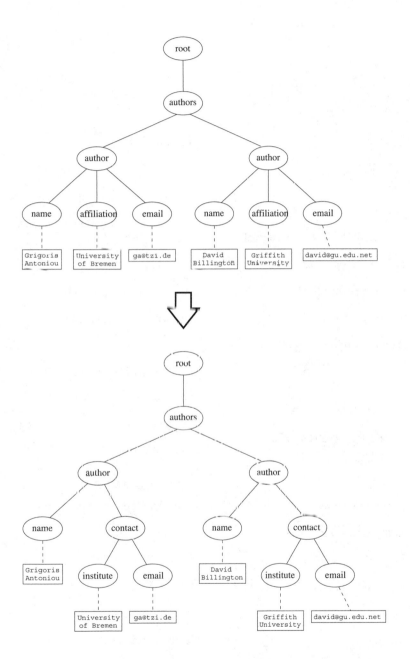

Figure A.6: XSLT as tree transformation

Index